Where are the Physicians?

Where are the Physicians?

◆

Preventing A Physician Shortage and Curtailed Healthcare Services

Lindsay L. Pratt, M.D.

iUniverse, Inc.
New York Lincoln Shanghai

Where are the Physicians?
Preventing A Physician Shortage and Curtailed Healthcare Services

iUniverse books may be ordered through booksellers or by contacting:

iUniverse
2021 Pine Lake Road, Suite 100
Lincoln, NE 68512
www.iuniverse.com
1-800-Authors (1-800-288-4677)

ISBN: 978-0-595-43303-2 (pbk)
ISBN: 978-0-595-87643-3 (ebk)

Printed in the United States of America

Contents

Preface

The year is 2015, and the public is asking, "Where are the physicians?" Also, they are complaining, "Why have my healthcare services become so difficult to obtain?"

The problem? There is a physician shortage, and the private healthcare delivery system has been replaced by a National Health Service. Also, the cost of the bureaucracy administering the National Health Service has required the public's healthcare's services to be curtailed.

Most individuals have not thought about either an impending physician shortage or the cost of a National Health Service requiring the public's healthcare's services to be curtailed. This book will have you rethinking those two issues as well as healthcare's other issues and problems. Also, it will outline how easily all of those issues and problems can be solved by six changes in the existing private healthcare delivery system. Furthermore, you will understand the importance of preserving a private healthcare delivery system, and the inherent dangers of allowing a National Health Service to replace our private healthcare delivery system.

Prior to legislation creating Medicare in the late 1960s and the managed healthcare industry in the mid 1970s neither were part of the healthcare delivery system. But since the 1990s, both have become healthcare's major insurers. The problem they pose for future physicians is their policies indicate neither plan to remain healthcare's insurers. Instead, they intend to control the healthcare delivery system.

The probability of government and the managed healthcare industry controlling healthcare has an increasing number of physicians concerned they, like the teachers in our government controlled education system, will become the pawns of another government bureaucracy. Over the past two decades, Medicare's and the managed healthcare industry's policies have become increasingly unfriendly toward physicians, and many physicians no longer enjoy the practice of medicine. Many physicians are planning to leave their practice as soon as they are able to do so, and they no longer recommend becoming a physician to be a good career choice. Already, many of the best of our youth are losing interest in becoming physicians, and the number of applications to medical schools is decreasing.

Unless a physician friendly healthcare delivery system is reestablished, a physician shortage is inevitable, and, or, many of those who become physicians will not have come from the best of our youth. Why would a young person with the ability to choose any career of their choice elect to spend at least ten to twelve years studying to become a physician whose future is a salaried employee of, and subject to whims of, another government bureaucracy?

Few among the public are aware of the reasons for the impending shortage of physicians, and few are aware of how serious a physician shortage would be for themselves and for their families. Therefore, regardless of your thoughts about physicians, everyone needs to rethink the importance of a physician to the future quality and availability of theirs, and their family's, healthcare services.

Physicians have valid reasons to fear government's desire is to control the healthcare delivery system. Over the past five decades, members in Congress have been introducing legislation designed to offer it the opportunity to enter the healthcare delivery system. Beginning in the 1950s, a group in Congress proposed legislation creating a National Health Service similar to England's, but they were not successful. However, in the late 1960s, legislation created both Medicare and Medicaid. This legislation offered those Congresspersons their opportunity to enter healthcare. But after entering healthcare, they found most of the public was satisfied with their private health insurance and with the private healthcare delivery system. To achieve their goal of a National Health Service, both the private health insurance industry and the private healthcare delivery system had to be destroyed. Both were successfully destroyed by legislation creating the managed healthcare industry (HMOs and multi-hospital systems) in the mid 1970s. (Addendum III)

Congress had no problem enacting HMO legislation. There was an apathetic public, and there were many businessperson and investors eager to enter healthcare. During the 1960s, unregulated health and hospital insurance money was flowing into the healthcare delivery system, and it was attracting those businesspersons and investors. They saw the opportunity to obtain large profits, but they had no way of entering healthcare. Congress, seeking a way to destroy both the private health insurance industry and the private healthcare delivery system, recruited their support, and together, they sponsored legislation in the mid 1970s creating the managed healthcare industry. Since the industry's entrance into healthcare, it has been assisting Congress to destroy both the private health insurance industry and the private healthcare delivery system.

The private insurance industry was destroyed by the managed healthcare industry's less expensive premiums. The private insurance industry was insuring everyone, even those individuals with a chronic illness and with disabilities. However, the HMOs were enrolling only healthy individuals. (Addendum III) Enrolling only healthy individuals provided HMOs the opportunity to offer less expensive premiums. During the 1980s, those premiums attracted an increasing number of the indemnity insurance industry's healthy individuals to the HMOs. The loss of their premiums created a cost problem for the private indemnity insurance industry. Their premiums had been paying some of the more expensive services required by the indemnity insurance industry's policyholders with chronic illnesses and disabilities. The need to continue to provide those expensive services without the healthy individual's premiums required the cost of the indemnity insurance industry's premiums to increase. Over a few decades, those premiums became less competitive with the HMO's premiums, and by the 1990s, the managed healthcare industry had replaced the private indemnity insurance industry as a major healthcare insurer.

Along with the destruction of the private indemnity insurance industry, the increasing number of HMO enrollees and Medicare patients were destroying the private healthcare delivery system. By the 1990s, HMO enrollees and Medicare patients had become the majority of patients, and healthcare's providers were forced to accept them along with their unfriendly provider policies.

After using the HMO industry to destroy both the private insurance industry and the private healthcare delivery system, those in Congress seeking a National Health Service attempted to destroy the HMO industry to obtain its infrastructure. This was to be accomplished by the "Patient's Bill of Right" legislation proposed in the 1990s. This unsuccessful legislation would have had HMO enrollees suing their HMOs. The cost of defending themselves from a flood of frivolous enrollee lawsuits would have forced the HMO industry into bankruptcy. To accommodate the large number of disfranchised HMO enrollees, Congress would have been "forced" to incorporate the HMO enrollees and its infrastructure into its proposed National Health Service.

Hopefully, a National Health Service, whose services are offered by the managed healthcare industry, will never become the healthcare delivery system in the United States. However, establishing a National Health Service remains a legislative priority among many in Congress. (Clinton Healthcare Legislation proposed in the early 1990s)

There is a reason why physicians need to be concerned about the probability of government controlling healthcare. The misuse of health and hospital insurance by many physicians over several decades has caused healthcare's costs to increase far more rapidly than the rate of inflation. Someone had to challenge those increasing healthcare costs, and the someone became government.

There are numerous indicators government will achieve its goal of controlling healthcare within this decade. There is a disorganized medical profession; there is the government's quest for the enormous political power offered by its controlling the healthcare delivery system; there are profits for the managed healthcare industry and its investors when they become the delivery system for the National Health Service; there is the increasing number of Medicare patients dependent on government for their healthcare services; and there is an increasing number of individuals easily influenced by misinformation. Much misinformation is being offered about healthcare's problems by the many special interest groups seeking healthcare's unregulated dollars, and an increasing number of individuals are being influenced by the misinformation. I do not recall to whom I need to give the credit, but an article I read several years ago discussed how the increasing loss of independent thinkers among our population is resulting in our Republic being lost from within. Since the 1950s, our government's many social programs have demanded nothing of, or expected anything from, a large segment of our population. With no expectations of themselves, those individuals have become dysfunctional, and they are easily influenced by misinformation. In contrast, individuals receiving government assistance during the 1930s were expected to, and were given, work such as the W.P.A. and the C.C.C .. Those individuals were productive, and they had expectations of themselves. They did not become dysfunctional, and they raised the "Greatest Generation" of men and women.

Another reason given for the increasing number of individuals influenced by misinformation is the failure of our government controlled public education system. The system has demanded nothing of, or expected anything from, too many of our youth. The system's standards have been lowered, and the system has not required every student to acquire an education before graduating.

As I recall, the article's number of dysfunctional from our country's many social programs was about 20% of our population, and from the poorly educated, an additional 20%. Those many dysfunctional individuals will respond to misinformation, and they will parrot and support whatever they are told will benefit them regardless of its authenticity or consequences. Using misinformation, government can obtain support from those dysfunctional individuals for its National Health Service. Hopefully, the remaining 60% of our population will obtain the information necessary for them to recognize the inherent dangers of a National Health Service.

To assist the 60% of our population to make an informed decision about the character of our country's future healthcare delivery system, this book discusses six changes to REGULATE the existing private healthcare delivery system. The regulation will provide the necessary reductions in healthcare's costs; will preserve a private healthcare delivery system; will provide EVERYONE healthcare services, even those unable to pay for them; and will provide services more comprehensively and more easily available than the services offered by either a National Health Service or the managed healthcare industry's HMOs and multi-hospital systems.

The six changes were introduced in my article that was not accepted for publication in 1988 and again in a manuscript "Reforming Healthcare. What the Public Needs To Know". The timing of those articles was wrong. At the time of their introduction, unchallenged insurance misusages were providing healthcare's providers large incomes, and they did not feel threatened by either government or the managed healthcare industry. In addition, the ability to misuse health and hospital insurance was making the public happy. They were requesting and receiving many "free" and unnecessary services. Hopefully, in 2007, this book will have the public and physicians rethinking their many health insurance misusages and how those misusages have provided government and the managed healthcare industry the opportunity to enter, and to seek the control of, the healthcare delivery system. The reasons why neither a government nor a managed healthcare industry controlled healthcare delivery system will benefit patients are discussed in this book.

Both a shortage of physicians and curtailed of healthcare services can be prevented by maintaining a physician friendly healthcare delivery system. Adopting the six changes proposed in this book to REGULATE the existing private healthcare delivery offers the best opportunity to insure a physician friendly healthcare delivery system prevails.

Unfortunately, too many individuals appear to have given no thought to the probability of either a physician shortage or curtailed healthcare services. Why? Eighty percent of our population is healthy. They are rarely sick, and they have not had the need to think about healthcare issues. But, those individuals have to be reminded: some type of serious illness awaits us all. At that time, an adequate number physicians who have come from the best of our youth will be important to them, and to their families.

Introduction

The year is 2013, and legislation has replaced the private healthcare delivery system with a National Health Service. During both the 2008 Presidential election and the 2010 Congressional midterm elections, the cost of healthcare's services had become a major political issue. Following those elections, the rhetoric from both those in Congress seeking to replace the private healthcare delivery system and from a bias media was receiving increasing public support. Public support was coming from an increasing number of people dependent on government for their healthcare services (Medicare), and from the increasing number of people no longer able to afford health and hospital insurance. In addition, no alternative healthcare delivery system had been proposed to offer business less expensive employee healthcare benefits, and business was offering its support for a National Health Service.

By the 2012 elections, most of the public considered a National Health Service to be an attractive alternative healthcare delivery system, and by 2013, Congress had the support it needed to enact legislation creating the National Health Service. As expected, the managed healthcare industry became the delivery system for the National Health Service.

In 2015, a shortage of physicians was beginning to become a problem. During the two preceding decades, the healthcare delivery system had become less and less physician friendly. An increasing number of physicians had either retired or limited their practices. Others had entered other healthcare careers. Also, the practice of medicine had lost its appeal, and becoming a physician was no longer an attractive career choice. Applications to medical schools were declining, and many of those individuals training to become physicians were not coming from the best of our youth.

In 2017, you have not been feeling well. You called the HMO you have been assigned and were told an appointment with your primary care physician could not be obtained for three weeks; however, you could come to the HMO's Walk-in Clinic and be examined by a physician's assistant.

The Walk-in Clinic is located in the emergency room of the managed healthcare industry's hospital in your area. When you arrive, there are many patients in the Clinic's waiting room. A receptionist interviews you and makes the decision you do not require immediate care. You are told to have a seat in the waiting room. When your name is called, you are triaged by a nurse followed by a physician assistant's examination. The decision is no medicine or additional examinations are necessary. You are sent home, and like many other patients that day, a physician did not examine you.

After several weeks of treatment for hip pain, the HMO's physician assistant referred your father to the HMO's primary care physician. The primary care physician referred your father to an Orthopedic surgeon. After waiting three months for the appointment, the Orthopedic surgeon recommended a hip replacement. However, the HMO's waiting period for the surgery, and for other elective surgical procedures, was several months. In addition to the scheduling delay, the HMO scheduled the hospital in which the surgery was to be performed. Also, the HMO assigned the surgeon to perform the surgery—a different Orthopedic surgeon than the one who had examined the patient initially.

Your neighbor told you she had been attempting for several weeks to obtain a referral from her HMO's physician assistant to her primary care physician. When she finally obtained the referral, the primary care physician told your neighbor she required a neurosurgical consultation. However, an appointment with a Neurosurgeon was not available for several months. Your neighbor was given a sheet of paper listing several symptoms and was instructed to return to her area's Walk in Clinic if any of the symptoms appeared. A determination of her need for an immediate neurosurgical referral would be made at the time.

In 2017, physician consultations, as well as many medical and surgical services, have become increasingly difficult to obtain. The difficulty in obtaining those consultations is a physician shortage. The difficulty obtaining the medical and surgical services is because those services have had to be curtailed. The bureaucracies administering both the National Health Service and the managed healthcare industry's HMOs and multi-hospital systems have become very expensive. Their costs leave fewer healthcare dollars available to purchase healthcare services for patients.

In addition to a physician shortage and curtailed healthcare services, additional taxes were required in 2016 to support the bureaucracies administering the National Health Service and the managed healthcare industry. Also, as predicted, those increasing taxes were creating an economic recession with increasing unemployment.

You ask in 2017, "What has happened?" Remember back in 2007 when you were told replacing the private healthcare delivery system with a National Health Service would cause a physician shortage. Also, you were warned the cost of the bureaucracies required to manage a National Health Service and the managed healthcare industry would leave fewer healthcare dollars available to purchase services for patients. Healthcare's services would have to be curtailed, and the comprehensive and easily obtained services previously offered by the private healthcare delivery system would no longer be available.

Also, in 2007, you were told Medicare's and the managed healthcare industry's policies were becoming increasingly hostile towards physicians, and you were told neither a National Health Service nor the managed healthcare industry could provide the career incentives necessary to attract the best from our youth to consider becoming physicians. In addition, you were told supporting a National Health Service would require taxes to be increased, and those increase taxes would be followed by a recession and increasing unemployment. Also, in 2007, you were told an abusive and frivolous malpractice litigation system had become insufferable and its costs unconscionable. Yet, you, and others, did nothing. Now, in 2017, there is a physician shortage and your healthcare services have had to be curtailed. You are asking, "Where are the Physicians?" and you are complaining, "Why have my healthcare services become difficult to obtain?"

Your neighbor had difficulty obtaining a consultation with a Neurosurgeon because there are only a few Neurosurgeons in 2017. Back in 2007, the cost of a Neurosurgeon's malpractice insurance was at least $90,000 to $100,000, and frivolous neurosurgical malpractice lawsuits were frequent. Prior to 2007, the number of Neurosurgeons in the United States had been around 3,500. However, in 2007, the number had become fewer than 2,500, and the number had continued to decrease until in 2017 there is a serious shortage of Neurosurgeons. In addition to Neurosurgeons, there is a serious shortage of other physicians. Why? Why become a physician and be harassed by government, by the managed healthcare industry, and by attorneys?

In addition to an unfriendly healthcare delivery system, healthcare's major insurers (Medicare and the managed healthcare industry) were reducing their insurance reimbursements to physicians. By 2010, physician incomes had been reduced significantly. In addition, the unconscionable cost of defending many frivolous malpractice lawsuits had become unacceptable. BUT attorneys were securing their incomes from malpractice litigation with their legislation mandating practicing physicians have malpractice insurance. Again, I ask, "Why consider becoming a physician?"

An example of the impact of reduced insurance reimbursements on physician incomes is the following study of hourly wages published in the Camden County Medical Society's Executive Committee's minutes, June 7, 2005. "—a weekend agency nurse makes $50/hr. The estimated hourly wages of several specialists were also calculated. Family Practice was $47.28, Internal Medicine was $51.38, Neurology was $63.00, OBGYN was $79.58, General Surgery was $83.74, ENT was $84.99, and Cardiology was $96.31—this was done in 2003, and insurance reimbursements have gone down. As horrific as this seems, in 2003, the hourly wage of a managed healthcare CEO was $1,423/hr."

A recent story told to me by a physician is another example of how insurance reimbursement policies are causing physicians to leave the practice of medicine and no longer recommend becoming a physician to be a good career choice. A young relative was in the area on business, and the physician and his wife took him to dinner. During dinner, the physician learned his relative was considering accepting another job in the area to increase his income. The physician's comment to me was, "My relative's income was already larger than mine. With all of my bills, with the stress of my practice, and with my decreasing income, why did I spend all of those years studying to be a physician? I'd have been better off using my brain in the business world, as my relative has done, and with much less educational preparation and stress."

Again, I ask, "Why become a physician?"

Allowing the private healthcare delivery system to collapse will not benefit the public. Its collapse benefits only those Congresspersons seeking a National Health Service and those investors in, and lobbyists for, the managed healthcare industry. Its collapse offers both of them the opportunity to control healthcare.

Control offers politicians enormous power and the managed healthcare industry easy profits. Observe the power of the welfare voting blocks in every large city. A National Health Service voting block would be much larger and more powerful. In addition to political power, a National Health Service would increase public dependency on government—the goal of many members in Congress. Also, since there will always be patients with the need for healthcare's services, and since insurance will always provide payment for those services, becoming the delivery system for the National Health Service will provide the managed healthcare industry easy profits. Furthermore, controlling the healthcare delivery system offers government and the managed healthcare industry the opportunity they have been seeking to establish the value of, and the reimbursements for, healthcare's services.

Another problem with a National Health Service is it creates another self serving and politically driven government bureaucracy. Like all bureaucracies, satisfying its needs will take precedence over the needs of those it administers. Also, all bureaucracies have difficulty providing the career incentives necessary to attract, and to retain, the best individuals to provide its services. In addition, bureaucracies always grow in size, power, and costs, and as their size, power, and costs increase, the availability of their services decreases.

The education bureaucracy in the United States is an example of an out-of-control self-serving government bureaucracy. Satisfying its needs requires the bureaucracy to consume an estimated 55% of education's dollars, and those "administrative" dollars never reach either the classrooms or the teachers. Also, each year the bureaucracy expresses its need for more dollars, and each year the quality of its services decreases. Furthermore, the education bureaucracy has NOT been able to offer the career incentives necessary to attract enough of our youth to become teachers or to retain enough qualified teachers for its classrooms. In addition, it has protected the inadequacies of many teachers, and too many students have not been required to obtain a good education prior to their graduation.

Hopefully, the government will never have the opportunity to do what it has done to our education system to our healthcare delivery system.

The following are facts the public needs to consider as they ponder the consequences of a government sponsored healthcare delivery system.

1. The probability is the profit driven managed healthcare industry's HMOs and multi-hospital systems will become the delivery system for a National Health Service. Why healthcare is not a business and why the managed healthcare industry should not become the delivery system in the United States is discussed in Addenda II and III.

2. Neither government nor the managed healthcare industry can provide a better delivery system than, or improve the services offered by, the existing private healthcare delivery system.

3. Neither government nor the managed healthcare industry can provide the career incentives necessary to attract the best of our youth to become physicians.

4. Government can sponsor a National Health Service, and the managed healthcare industry can offer the public their healthcare services, but neither possesses the ability to PROVIDE those services. Physicians are necessary to provide those services. Also, the quality of those services will depend on the abilities of the physicians providing them, and the availability of those services will depend on the number of physicians available to provide them.

5. Insurance will remain the payment system for healthcare's services regardless of the delivery system offering those services. But, the services purchased by insurance will be meaningless without an adequate supply of qualified physicians to provide them.

6. Patients over the age of 55 consume about 65% or more of healthcare's services, and their number is increasing. A delivery system's ability to attract and retain enough qualified physicians to provide those services must become a healthcare priority.

7. The rhetoric from unhappy practicing physicians and the threat of a National Health Service has our youth questioning careers as physician.

8. Endorsing the six changes proposed in this book to REGULATE the existing private healthcare delivery system offers the best opportunity to provide the

career incentives necessary to attract the best of our youth to consider become physicians. Those incentives are:

a. The opportunity to be independent practitioners in a private fee-for-service healthcare delivery system instead of salaried employees in a National Health Service and the managed healthcare industry.

b. The opportunity to have their insurance reimbursements calculated by the Provider Reimbursement Formula, discussed in Chapter 5, instead of calculated by self-serving healthcare insurers.

c. The opportunity to have ALL of healthcare's dollars spent purchasing healthcare's services rather than spent supporting the bureaucracies administering a National Health Service and the managed healthcare industry. (Addendum V)

d. The opportunity to treat patients who have had the freedom to select the providers of their choice.

e. The opportunity to determine the services required by their patients without an insurance company's approval prior to their patient receiving them. (Chapter 4)

f. The opportunity to offer their patients more comprehensive, better quality, and more easily available healthcare services, at a lower cost than the services offered by a National Health Service.

Why would independent thinking people consider replacing the private healthcare delivery system with a National Health Service? The ability of any "system" to attract an adequate number of the best individuals to the "system" depends on the career incentives offered by the "system". Over the past several decades, neither government's (Medicare) nor the managed healthcare industry's delivery systems have provided those career incentives. Accordingly, their ability to attract an adequate number of the best of our youth to become our future physicians has to be questioned. In contrast, a private healthcare delivery system provides those career incentives, and it offers the best opportunity to have a delivery system offering the necessary career incentives.

Before offering support for a National Health Service whose services are offered the public by the managed healthcare industry, the public needs to think about the following:

1. Am I going to be satisfied when my healthcare services become increasingly more difficult to obtain?

2. Am I going to be satisfied when a third party tells me when, where, and from whom I will receive my services?

3. Am I going to be satisfied when the quality and comprehensiveness of my services become inferior to the services I'm now receiving?

4. Am I going to be satisfied when a politically driven bureaucracy administers a National Health Service that offers me services from the lowest-bid managed healthcare company?

5. Am I going to be satisfied when 50%, or more, of my healthcare dollars are no longer purchasing healthcare services for patients? Instead, they are supporting the cost of the healthcare bureaucracies administering both a National Health Service and the managed healthcare industry. (Addenda V and Healthcare's Insurers.)

6. Am I going to be satisfied with services provided by physicians who have come from among the best of our youth?

7. Or, are the many benefits I have received from the private healthcare delivery system worth preserving?

Yes, the existing private healthcare delivery system has its cost and its service availability problems for those people unable to pay for their healthcare services. But both of those problems have been created by the misuse of unregulated health and hospital insurance, and those insurance misusages can be corrected by the six changes proposed in this book to regulate the existing private healthcare delivery system.

1

The Problem, The Cause, and The Solution

I entered medicine in 1949, and as the end of the 1980s approached, I began to think about my retirement. Over many years, I had no need to think about what was happening to the practice of medicine. As a salaried member of several University Medical School Staffs, I had been shielded from the problems surfacing in medicine. But, the closure of the free clinics and hospital wards in the early 1970s, made me aware the practice of medicine was changing, and in 1988, when I became the President of our Medical Society, I began to examine those changes. What I found was a disappointment. The practice of medicine I had known and enjoyed was rapidly disappearing.

I had known the practice of medicine to be a patient driven profession whose mission was to provide services to all in need of those services regardless of their ability to pay. However, the introduction of employer and government sponsored health and hospital insurance during the 1950s had transformed the patient driven practice of medicine into an insurance driven for-profit business system called the healthcare delivery system. Its mission was to provide healthcare's services to only those individuals who could afford to purchase them. In addition, the role of the physician had been abased. The "practice of medicine" had become the "healthcare delivery system".

The Problem.

The only problem with healthcare has been, and remains, its unconscionable cost.

The Cause.

The only cause of healthcare's unconscionable costs has been, and remains, the patient, physician, and other healthcare provider misusages of health and hospital insurance.

During the 1950s and into 1960s, employers began to offer their employees hospital and health insurance, and in the late 1960s, legislation created Medicare and Medicaid. By the 1970s, most everyone had some type of health and hospital insurance. Prior to those insurance programs, the private healthcare delivery system had neither a cost nor a service availability problem.

When I entered medicine in 1949, the patient's pocketbook was the primary source of payment for medical and surgical services. Those patients who could afford to purchase their services questioned their medical necessity, and they purchased only necessary services. Those patients who could not afford to purchase their services were able to obtain free services in outpatient clinics and in inpatient hospital wards. For more than twenty years, I taught medical students and resident physicians surgery in those free clinics and hospital wards. I know the services offered those patients were of better quality and more easily obtained than most of the services offered to Medicaid patients and to patients unable to pay for their services by the existing insurance driven private healthcare delivery system.

Unfortunately, those health and hospital insurance programs were not regulated, and as increasing numbers of individuals began to use their insurance to purchase their healthcare services during the 1960s and 1970s, healthcare's costs began to increase. Insurance programs were not monitoring either the medical necessity of, or the charges for, the services they were purchasing.

Without a challenge from their insurance companies, patients began to demand more and more healthcare services and to demand their insurance pay for those additional services. Patients became indifferent to the medical necessity of, and the cost of, their services. They were demanding and accepting healthcare services more for their convenience and desirability than for their medical necessity.

Without a challenge from either their patients or their patient's insurance companies, physicians, and other healthcare providers, began to offer patients the medically unnecessary services they were requesting, to charge more for their services, and to charge for services they had been offering without a charge prior to insurance. Furthermore, providers began to maximize their insurance reimbursements by unbundling (itemizing) their service charges, and neither insurance profiteering nor fraudulent insurance claims were being challenged. In addition, some healthcare providers were employing lobbyists to acquire legislation mandating insurance programs pay for their services even though those services may not have had a known medical value.

The patient and provider misuse of health and hospital insurance during the late 1960s and into the 1970s was generating billions of insurance dollars, and as those dollars flowed into the healthcare delivery system, they inflated healthcare's costs from less than 5% of the GNP in 1970 to more than 15% in the 1980s. Also, as those billions of insurance dollars flowed into healthcare, they provided healthcare's providers with "deep pockets". Those "deep pockets" attracted attorneys. By the 1980s, the cost of defending an increasing number of frivolous malpractice lawsuits had become unconscionable. Provider fees had to be increased to pay for those increasing malpractice insurance costs.

In addition to fostering attorney, patient, and healthcare provider solecism and chicanery, increasing healthcare costs was preventing an increasing number of self-employed individuals and small companies from purchasing health and hospital insurance. With free healthcare service facilities no longer available, those patients with no insurance found obtaining their healthcare services increasingly difficult. Insurance had conjured the idea among too many physicians, and other healthcare providers, they no longer had to provide their services without payment. In addition, some providers used collection agencies to collect their fees form patients who were unable to pay them.

Using collection agencies to collect unpaid bills in a free market economy is appropriate. In a free market economy, the individual had the option of deciding whether or not they wanted to purchase the service. However, in healthcare, a patient does not have the option of deciding whether or not they want to purchase a necessary healthcare service. They must receive it. Therefore, using collection agencies to collect unpaid bills for necessary healthcare services from those individuals without the financial resources to pay for them is not appropriate.

Along with the service availability issues for patients unable to pay for their services, increasing health and hospital insurance costs were creating economic problems for our country. One problem was the loss of the many better paying manufacturing jobs. The increasing cost of their employee's healthcare benefits was forcing many manufacturers to seek less expensive manufacturing opportunities outside of the United States. Otherwise, their products would not be competitive in the global economy.

If the United States is to retain its manufacturing economy, and if those manufactured products are to remain competitive in the present global economy, healthcare's costs must be reduced to an Internationally competitive 8% to 9% of our GNP. The recommendations in this book will accomplish that goal.

The Solution.

Adopting the six changes proposed in this book to REGULATE the existing private healthcare delivery system will solve healthcare's costs and service availability problems. The six changes regulate the charges for, and the utilization of, healthcare's services.

There will be many challenges to their acceptance. Special interest groups, like the managed healthcare industry, will be seeking to maintain their share of healthcare's unregulated insurance dollars. Another challenge can be expected from political interests seeking control of the healthcare delivery system. Hopefully, this book will awaken the public to the importance of a regulated private healthcare delivery system and the medical profession to the importance of their adopting the six changes as their agenda to challenge their many adversaries.

The six changes are:

1. Litigation reforms.

2. Monitoring all patient's services for their medical necessity.

3. Changing how provider insurance reimbursements are calculated and awarded—The Provider Reimbursement Formula.

4. Co-payments.

5. Regulating the charges a hospital can apply as a fixed cost and monitoring a hospital's variable costs.

6. Restoring the free outpatient clinic s and inpatient wards that existed prior to the 1970s.

2

Litigation Reforms

The litigation reform is the first of the six changes proposed to regulate the existing private healthcare delivery system. Their discussion is first because their endorsement and adoption is necessary if the goals of the other five changes are to be achieved.

Unfortunately, an apathetic and poorly informed public appears to be neither concerned with, nor unaware of, our country's irresponsible and out-of-control litigation system. The public appears to consider initiating a lawsuit to be the same as purchasing a lottery ticket. I'll initiate a lawsuit and hope I'll win. It will cost me nothing. WRONG! Those lawsuits are costing every person, and our country's economy, billions of dollars unnecessarily every year. Equally important is the increasing number of irresponsibly initiated malpractice lawsuits are causing the best of our youth to rethink becoming a physician.

Perhaps a historical perspective will illustrate how malpractice litigation became a problem and why the public's support for legislation reforming malpractice litigation is necessary.

Prior to the 1960s, medical malpractice lawsuits were rare. At the time, the patient's pocketbook was the primary source of payment for healthcare's services. Neither physicians nor hospitals had "deep pockets". However, during the 1960s, unregulated health and hospital insurance money was flowing into the healthcare delivery system, and both healthcare's providers and hospitals acquired "deep pockets". Those "deep pockets" attracted attorneys who recognized rapidly that the practice of medicine was not a "black and white" science. Instead, it abounds in "gray areas", and those "gray areas" would provide attorneys an advantage in malpractice lawsuits. Jury members selected from among the general population would have difficulty understanding those "gray areas".

My experience with malpractice litigation is an example of how the frequency of lawsuits increased following insurance providing physicians "deep pockets". I entered medicine in 1949, and my first malpractice lawsuit was not until around 1975. But, from 1975 to 1985, I had four frivolous malpractice lawsuits. Two were found to have no malpractice during depositions, and juries found the other two lawsuits to have no malpractice.

The most discouraging aspect of my lawsuits was their origin. Clinic (Medicaid) patients initiated three of them. For more than twenty years, I had enjoyed treating clinic patients while teaching surgery. But after they acquired Medicaid in the late 1960s, the mindset of many of them changed. They began to initiated malpractice lawsuits with increasing frequency, and the increasing numbers of those lawsuits are why many physicians refused to provide those patients services.

During the 1970s and into the 1980s, the number of malpractice lawsuits began to increase significantly, and by the 1980s, the cost of defending them was estimated to be at least 50 billion dollars. In addition to those 50 billion defense dollars, additional billions of dollars were required to pay for the many unnecessary services physicians were forced to offer their patients to protect themselves from frivolous lawsuits. Both the increasing cost of defending malpractice lawsuits and the increasing cost of the healthcare services required to protect physicians from frivolous lawsuits increased healthcare's costs significantly during the 1980s.

An example of a frivolous lawsuit was one I experienced as a member of a hospital's Board of Trustees. A patient was suing a member of the hospital's Medical Staff. The hospital had approved the physician's credentials; therefore, the hospital was included in the patient's lawsuit. In addition, since the Board of Trustees had approved the hospital's approval of the physician's credentials, each member of the Board of Trustees was included in the lawsuit. The lawsuit was proven to be frivolous, but the cost of defending the physician, the hospital, and each member of the Board of Trustees was enormous.

The public's complacency about, and indifference to, malpractice reform legislation has made the healthcare delivery system a captive of an out-of-control litigation system. Wake up America!!! It is YOUR healthcare delivery system being destroyed, and only you hold the key to obtaining the legislation necessary to reform malpractice litigation. The public's key is the power of their vote. Legislators want to be elected and reelected, and successful elections require the public's vote. Since attorneys dominate state legislatures, and since malpractice litigation is very profitable for those attorneys, obtaining the necessary malpractice reform legislation will be impossible without an informed public using the power of their vote to force legislators to enact appropriate malpractice legislation.

The trial lawyer's lobby is aware of the public's voting power, and it is spending much money promoting misinformation about litigation. Some of the misinformation is discussed in the next chapter.

Perhaps one reason for the public's complacency about initiating the necessary malpractice reform legislation is they are neither aware of, nor do they understand, the four major problems with existing malpractice litigation. An awareness of those four problems should move more individuals to offer their support for malpractice reform legislation. The four major problems are:

1. The absence of financial accountability.

2. The cost of defense.

3. The jury system.

4. The court system tolerating frivolous lawsuits .

Financial Accountability.

Patients can initiate malpractice lawsuits without any cost to themselves. But the physician or hospital being sued must bear the cost of employing the attorneys necessary to defend themselves. Furthermore, the physician or hospital being sued is unable to recover any of their defense costs after successfully defending themselves.

Persons initiating unsuccessful malpractice lawsuits must be made accountable for the financial damages their lawsuit has caused those they have sued. Since initiating an unsuccessful lawsuit incurs no expense for those initiating the lawsuit, too many frivolous malpractice lawsuits are initiated in the United States.

Defense Costs.

Defending malpractice lawsuits is an enormous expense for physicians, hospitals, and other healthcare providers, but those lawsuits are very profitable for attorneys. Therefore, attorneys can be expected to vigorously and disingenuously oppose any change in the existing litigation system. The present system is a win-win for attorneys. Attorneys initiating lawsuits profit from either a settlement made to prevent additional litigation expense or from a large percentage of an award. Other attorneys profit defending lawsuits.

A fact! Defending most malpractice lawsuits is an unnecessary expense for both physicians and hospitals. No malpractice was identified in approximately 70% to 80% of the malpractice lawsuits I was asked to review during the 1980s and 1990s. Other physicians have found the same number of unnecessary lawsuits. Also, juries have found similar numbers of no malpractice following jury trials. However, attorneys find defending those unnecessary lawsuits to be very profitable. In the 1980s, I was informed by an insurance company about 60 or 65 cents of every dollar hospitals and physicians paid for their malpractice insurance was paid to the attorneys the insurance company had to employ to defend them.

The cost of defending 70% or 80% of present malpractice lawsuits is unnecessary because they are "maloccurrence" lawsuits. What is maloccurrence? All of the procedures, studies, tests, etc. used to either evaluate or treat patients for their illnesses and disorders may result in an unsatisfactory outcome. If the unsatisfactory outcome is caused by negligence, there is malpractice. However, if everything was done properly, and there is an unsatisfactory outcome, there is maloccurrence. In my experience, at least 70% to 80% of malpractice lawsuits are maloccurrence lawsuits.

The Jury System

The selection of jury members from among the general population is another problem with existing malpractice litigation. An individual is supposed to be judged by a jury of their peers. The present selection of jurors from among the general population does not offer physicians or hospitals the opportunity to be judged by a jury of their peers.

A special court needs to be established for malpractice litigation, and the jurors in those special courts need to be at least three physicians who provide the same services as those in the lawsuit and who were appointed by a Medical Society in a different community than the one in which the physician or hospital being sued is located.

Tolerating Frivolous Lawsuits.

The increasing number of unnecessary malpractice lawsuits is the result of a court system tolerating those unnecessary lawsuits. To justify those lawsuits, the court has said, "The public is entitled to their day in court". Every individual is entitled to their day in court; however, the individual has to be made responsible for the content of their lawsuit and accountable for the defense costs of those they have sued if their lawsuit is not successful.

The Proposed Litigation Reforms.

The proposed litigation reforms are fair to both those individuals initiating lawsuits and to those individuals being sued, and their endorsement will benefit both. They are:

1. The attorney contingency fee will be retained.
No one should be denied the opportunity to initiate a valid lawsuit because of their inability to pay the fee of the attorney of their choice.

2. Malpractice Review Committees.
Local Medical and Osteopathic Societies will establish Malpractice Review Committees. All malpractice lawsuits will be referred to a Committee located in a different community than the one in which the physician being sued has their practice. Hospitals have the option of referring their lawsuits to a Society's Malpractice Review Committee located in a different community; however, the lawsuit must be about a physician's services.

3. Review Teams.
The Society's Committee will appoint at least two local physicians to a Malpractice Review Team. Team members will provide the same services as those contained in the lawsuit.

The Team's review of a lawsuit offers the physician being sued the opportunity to have their lawsuit reviewed by a jury of their peers. Also, Team members can provide jury members more objective information about the difference between maloccurrence and negligence than can an expert witness. Expert witnesses function as "hired guns" for the attorneys employing them. I have witnessed jurors confused by the conflicting testimonies of expert witnesses representing each side of a lawsuit.

Objections to Team members reviewing lawsuits have focused on Team members protecting the physician or hospital being sued. After several years of reviewing, and participating in, malpractice lawsuits, the chance of a Team from a different community protecting a physician or hospital is far less than the protection offered by an expert witness employed by an attorney.

An example is when I had to testify against a physician. There was no maloccurrence. There was negligence. However, the attorney defending the physician had employed an expert witness who was more articulate than I. The jury members were mesmerized by his articulate presentation of many medical ambiguities, and the jury was convinced he was right and I was wrong. He was hired to do a "job", and he did it much better than I. My presentation lost the lawsuit, and a patient who deserved compensation for the damages caused by a physician's negligence received nothing.

Another problem with the expert witness system is their excessive charges. Although the expert witness in the previous lawsuit made an excellent presentation, he was very expensive. Team members would have been equally effective but much less expensive.

Team member's compensation will be paid by the insurance company representing the physician or hospital, and their payment would be calculated by the Provider Reimbursement Formula. (Discussed in Chapter 5).

All community physicians would be required to accept an assignment to their local Society's Malpractice Review Team regardless of whether or not they are members of the Society. The penalty for refusal to accept an assignment could be the refusal of an insurance company to offer future malpractice insurance to the physician who refused a Team assignment.

4. The Team members will review the medical records, and their report will be referred to the Society's Malpractice Review Committee. The Committee sends the Team's report to both attorneys.

5. Both attorneys, as well as their expert witnesses, have the opportunity to question the Team members during a deposition.

6. If the lawsuit goes to a trial, the trial should to be held in a special malpractice court. As discussed previously, the jury members in those special courts would be at least three physicians who offer the same services as those in the lawsuit. Those physicians would be appointed by a Medical or Osteopathic Society located in a different community than the one in which the physician being sued has their practice. Also, the Team members who reviewed the lawsuit will have come from a different community.

The importance of Team members presenting their findings to a three physician jury in a special malpractice court is the need to have appropriate decisions made between negligence and maloccurrence. However, if the trial must be before a jury selected from among the general population, the Team would present their findings to the jury. Only the jury members and the judge could question the Team's members. A cross-examination of the Team members by either attorney in front of the jury would not be allowed. The attorneys, and their expert witnesses, had their opportunity to cross-examine the Team members during the deposition.

Following several years of providing testimony during jury trials, my observation of the purpose of an attorney's cross-examination of a witness is to discredit the witness and to confuse the jury. An experienced trial attorney can discredit most witnesses during cross-examinations. An example was one of my experiences. After several hours of my testimony defending a physician, the attorney said, "Doctor, how many grafts have you taken from this area?" I said, "Several." He said in a loud voice, "Doctor, you testified you had not taken grafts from the area." During my deposition one year previously I had said, "I have never taken a graft OF THIS SIZE from the area." The attorney had neglected to include "of this size" in his question to me. However, when I was required to take the time to review my deposition taken the previous year to find what I had said, the attorney had effectively made me appear confused. My testimony had been successfully discredited.

During another trial, I had to testify against a physician who was guilty of malpractice. The attorney spent at least twenty minutes asking me questions, such as, "How many times have I testified against physicians?" "Do I only testify against physicians?" "How much I charged?" "What percentage of my income comes from my testimonies against physicians?" etc. He successfully made me appear as a "bad guy" who testified against physicians for profit. Our patient lost their valid lawsuit.

7. The loser-pays-all policy.
Endorsing the loser-pays-all policy is a MUST if the many maloccurrence lawsuits are to be eliminated. The loser-pays-all policy neither denies an individual of their Constitutional right to initiate a lawsuit nor does it deny an individual of their opportunity to engage the attorney of their choice with no cost to themselves. The loser-pays-all policy only requires the individual initiating a lawsuit to be financially responsible for the defense costs of those they have sued if their lawsuit is not successful. This offers those who have been sued the opportunity to recover their defense costs after successfully defending themselves.

Attorneys will vigorously, relentlessly, and disingenuously oppose the loser-pays-all policy. It would require those individuals initiating lawsuits to evaluate the merits of their lawsuit more carefully. Since most malpractice lawsuits are maloccurrence lawsuits, at least 60% to 70% of present malpractice lawsuits would never be initiated. Although savings would be significant for healthcare's providers, the financial loss for attorneys would be in the billions of dollars. Also, fewer attorneys would be required to initiate and to defend malpractice lawsuits.

An additional benefit of the loser-pays-all policy is it offers patients with valid malpractice lawsuits a better opportunity to win their lawsuits. Attorneys encourage physicians guilty of malpractice to seek jury trials, and many of those physicians receive favorable jury decisions. However, if the loser-pays-all policy, along with the other recommended litigation reforms, were adopted, fewer physicians guilty of malpractice would be requesting jury trials in the hope of obtaining a favorable jury decision. First, a physician would know their peers from another community, and not a jury selected from among the general population, would be evaluating and judging the merits of their lawsuit. Second, the loser-pays-all policy would require the physician, and not the physician's insurance company, to pay the defense costs of those they have sued if their lawsuit were not successful. When a Team has established there is malpractice, and when a loser-pays-all policy requires the physician pay the court costs, a physician would be foolish not to settle their malpractice lawsuit rather than attempt to defend it. In terms of litigation costs, a physician's settlement would be less expensive than the cost of attorneys, depositions, and the other trial cost.

Four major problems with existing malpractice litigation have been discussed, and a rational and workable litigation reform program has been presented. Physicians, other healthcare providers, the business community, and the public will be the beneficiaries of the proposed reforms,. They are encouraged to endorse and support the proposed reforms.

3

Where is the Support For Malpractice Legislation?

Why has the public not offered support for medical malpractice reforms? The most probable reason is most of the public do not pay for their healthcare services. They have no idea of how much irresponsible malpractice lawsuits are increasing healthcare's costs. Also, the public is inundated with misinformation about our country's litigation system. For example, some individuals believe a change in the existing litigation system would block their Constitutional right to initiate a lawsuit. Wrong! The only requirement of the proposed malpractice reforms in Chapter 2 is to have the individual initiating a lawsuit be responsible for the content of their lawsuit and to have them pay any financial damages caused by their lawsuit if their lawsuit is not successful.

Misinformation is a problem. Too many people believe the existing litigation system is not a problem for them. Wrong! Every service and product in the United States has a significant litigation cost included in its cost. The cost of defending the many, too many, frivolous lawsuits is enormous. The cost of the many, too many, irresponsible jury awards is enormous. Also, the cost of the settlements forced upon individuals and companies to avoid additional litigation expenses is enormous. Yes, the existing litigation system creates a significant cost problem for everyone. Those costs are included in the price of every service or product purchased in the United States.

Misinformation has other individuals believing malpractice lawsuit costs are paid by insurance companies. Wrong! The public pays those costs. The only money insurance companies have is the public's money. It is the money insurance companies receive when their policyholders pay their premiums. In malpractice litigation, the insurance company's policyholders are physicians, and the money physicians use to pay their malpractice insurance premiums comes from their patients. Therefore, the money insurance companies use to pay the attorneys to defend physicians, to pay the malpractice litigation settlements and jury awards, and to pay other litigation expenses is the public's (patient's) money.

The lack of understanding about insurance issues among too many individuals is troubling. Recently, an individual was complaining about their homeowners insurance rate increasing so much in Florida. However, the same person announced several months ago the insurance had replaced all of the shingles on his roof after a few shingles had blown off during a recent storm.

The social and economic consequences of no malpractice reform in the United States are enormous, and they are getting worse. No other country has as many irresponsibly initiated lawsuits as those initiated in the United States. Our litigation system is out-of-control, and it MUST be reformed. Unfortunately, ONLY the vote of an informed public will obtain the appropriate reform legislation. But the public appears to have no interest in initiating those reforms. In the meantime, frivolous lawsuits will continue, and they will cause healthcare's costs to continue to increase, as well as the cost of the other products and services the public purchases in the United States. Equally important, those lawsuits are discouraging many of the best of our youth from seeking a career as a physician.

Can public support for malpractice reform be anticipated? Probably not! Initiating a lawsuit is easy and costs nothing. Unfortunately, there are too few independent thinkers who recognize how destructive the existing litigation system is to our country's economy. Also, they do not recognize the cost of defending frivolous lawsuits is forcing employers to transfer their manufacturing to other countries where the litigation system is more responsible than in the United States.

If the public had to pay for the increasing cost of healthcare's services, and if they were aware of how frivolous lawsuits were increasing the cost of those services, they would eagerly support litigation reforms. However, I am reminded of a fact. While many individuals discuss healthcare's costs, those costs are not an issue with them. Why? A misinformed public believes they do not pay those costs. Instead, their insurance, provided by others, pays those costs.

In another decade, the public will be witnessing meaningless political investigations into the causes of a physician shortage and curtailed healthcare services.

But, being attorneys, politicians will not identify a major reason for the shortage and curtailed services. But the truth will be the litigation harassment and the unconscionable cost of malpractice insurance have caused our youth to seek other careers.

A reminder: Although you may be one of the 80% of the population who are healthy, and who have not had the need to think about healthcare issues, but some serious illness is in your future. At that time, your physician's availability and abilities will be important!!

Offer your support for the recommended malpractice reforms. It's you healthcare delivery system! Defend it, or lose it.

4

Monitoring for Medical Necessity

Monitoring the services patients receive for their medical necessity is the second change to regulate the private healthcare delivery system.

Unnecessary services cost the healthcare delivery system billions of dollars each year, and those costs are second only to the cost of malpractice litigation. If the necessary reductions in healthcare's costs are to be achieved, the cost of unnecessary healthcare services must be eliminated. The proposed monitoring program will eliminate those unnecessary services. Equally important, the proposed monitoring program returns the responsibility for monitoring and eliminating those unnecessary services to local Medical and Osteopathic Societies where it once was, and where it belongs.

When "something" is free, there can never be enough of the "something", and the need for, the value of, and the cost of, the "something" never becomes a consideration for those receiving the "something". If patients were required to pay for their healthcare services, as they did prior to hospital and health insurance, they would not be accepting at least 30% to 40% of the services they are now receiving.

What is a medically necessary service? The service has to have a documented medical value, and it is NECESSARY to either diagnosis or treat an illness, a disorder, or a disease.

Prior to the 1960s, monitoring for medical necessity was not necessary. Patients paid for their services from their pocketbooks, and they questioned their medical necessity. Those patients who could not afford to purchase their services received medically necessary services in the free outpatient clinics and inpatient hospital wards.

Unnecessary services became a problem following the introduction of unregulated health and hospital insurance. Insurance companies were not monitoring the medical necessity of the services their policyholders were receiving, and without monitoring challenges, patients began to request, and provider began to provide, medically unnecessary services.

The first healthcare insurer to initiate medical necessity monitoring was Medicare. As Medicare's costs increased during the 1970s, Medicare began to monitor the medical necessity of the services Medicare and Medicaid patients were receiving. But there were problems with those monitoring programs, as well as with the monitoring programs of other healthcare insurers. Some of those problems were:

1. Monitoring by unqualified individuals.

2. The timing of the medical necessity decision.

3. Identifying a service with a known medical value, but prescribed unnecessarily.

4. Identifying a service to have no known medical value.

5. The absence of penalties for those providers offering, and patients requesting, unnecessary services.

6. Litigation.

    a. Healthcare's providers forced to provide unnecessary healthcare services, and

    b. lawsuits initiated by providers whose services were being monitored.

Monitoring by Unqualified Individuals

Medicare's medical necessity monitoring began in the 1970s. Medicare awarded contracts to individuals to establish Peer Review Organizations, referred to as the PROs. The PROs employed physicians and other healthcare providers to make medical necessity decisions about the services Medicare and Medicaid patients were receiving. However, one of PRO's problems was some of the individuals they employed were not qualified to make those decisions.

An example of an unqualified physician making PRO medical necessity decisions was the physician who denied ten days of hospitalization for one of my patients. A patient who had extensive surgery for cancer with reconstruction of the mouth and throat was having difficulty learning to swallow. His hospitalization was prolonged. The PROs denied ten days of the patient's hospitalization. When I attended the PRO's appeal hearing, I learned the surgeon who had monitored and denied the ten days of hospitalization had never performed a surgical procedure like the one I had performed. In addition, he was unable to describe the physiology of swallowing. Regardless of his inadequate knowledge of the operation, of the physiology of swallowing, and of the patient's recovery problems, the hospital was denied ten days of Medicare reimbursements.

Most of my patients required prolonged hospitalizations following their surgery, and after several bad experiences with PRO audits, I concluded, one of the PRO's problems was their use of unqualified individuals to make their medical necessity monitoring decisions.

Responsible medical necessity monitoring requires the individual monitoring the services of others to provide the same services as those they are asked to monitor. The best place to find those qualified individuals is in local Medical and Osteopathic Societies.

Prior to the 1970s, local Medical and Osteopathic Societies were able to effectively monitor the professional activities of community physicians, and those Societies were able to apply penalties to physicians offering medically unnecessary services. For example, around 1960, I had to appear before a local Society's monitoring committee to defend my insertion of tubes into children's ears to improve their hearing. There had been complaints from other community physicians who had not accepted the tubes as the standard of care. If I had not been able to defend my use of the tubes, I could have been censored. At the time, being censored could threaten my ability to obtain malpractice insurance and hospital staff privileges.

However, since the 1970s, lawsuits initiated by healthcare providers whose services were being monitored have forced local Societies to abandon their previously effective medical necessity monitoring. Also, since the physicians monitoring those services were frequently included in the provider's lawsuit, qualified physicians were refusing to accept monitoring assignments. Although

Societies and the monitoring physicians could successfully defend themselves, neither wanted the stress of a lawsuit, the cost of employing an attorney, or the inability to recover any of their defense costs. Until the recovery of defense costs is made possible with a loser-pays-all policy, the cost of having to defend lawsuits will limit, if not prevent, Medical and Osteopathic Societies from monitoring the medical necessity of many healthcare services provided by community physicians.

The Timing of a Medical Necessity Decision.

An HMO's attempt to adhere to a budget required it to deny enrollee's services before their enrollees received them. However, those denials compromised the treatment programs of too many enrollees.

Medical necessity decisions must NEVER be made prior to the patient receiving the service. Those decisions must always be made after the patient has received the service, and appropriate penalties applied at that time.

A Service With a Known Medical Value is Used Unnecessarily.

Another monitoring problem is when a service with a known medical value is used unnecessarily. An example is the use of an antibiotic to treat a virus infection. Antibiotics have a known medical value. They destroy bacteria. However, antibiotics do not destroy viruses. Therefore, when an antibiotic is used to treat a common cold (viral infection), it is medically unnecessary. But, when an antibiotic is used to treat a bacterial complication of a viral infection, the antibiotic is medically necessary.

Identifying a Service To Have No Known Medical Value.

There is a significant difference between identifying a service as having no medical NECESSITY and identifying a service as having no known medical VALUE. Medical necessity monitoring will be challenged when identifying a service to have no medical value, and no longer eligible to receive insurance reimbursements. A lawsuit is inevitable.

Patients are receiving, and insurance is paying for, many services that have no known medical value. Identifying those services and eliminating their insurance reimbursements would save millions of healthcare's dollars. However, eliminating those reimbursements will initiate many legal challenges. Anticipating those challenges, those services will not be identified in this book. Although their identification and elimination is necessary, the litigation reforms proposed in Chapter 2 must be active before anyone will attempt to identify a service as possessing no medial value and no longer eligible for insurance reimbursements.

When services are identified as medically unnecessary, the patient may continue to receive the service. However, their insurance will no longer pay for the service.

The Absence of Penalties.

Another reason medical necessity monitoring has not been successful is the absence of penalties for those patients requesting, and for those physicians, and other healthcare providers, providing, unnecessary services. If effective medical necessity monitoring is to be achieved, severe penalties are necessary for patients requesting, and for providers providing, medically unnecessary services.

Litigation.

Effective medical necessity monitoring will require the litigation reforms in Chapter 2 to be adopted. Why? The frequency of frivolous malpractice lawsuits forces physicians to offer their patients medically unnecessary services. Physicians know trial attorneys attempt to convince jury members the physician should have done "this" or ordered "that" rather than what the physician "did". Therefore, physicians want every possible test and procedure in the patient's record. The need to continue to provide those expensive and unnecessary services will continue until the litigation reforms proposed in Chapter 2 become active.

Another litigation problem is the lawsuit initiated by the physician, or other healthcare provider, whose service is being monitored. The lawsuit can be against the Medical or Osteopathic Society requesting the monitor, against the physician monitoring the services, or against both. The cost of an engaging an attorney and the inability to recover any of defense costs after a successful defense inhibits, and in too many instances prevents, effective monitoring for medical necessity.

An example of how litigation has impeded effective monitoring was one of my experiences. A member of the Medical Staff was performing services that I believed required monitoring. The hospital's administration had me express my concerns with the hospital's attorney. Avoiding the cost of defending an expensive lawsuit became the attorney's primary concern. Following my discussions with the attorney, the since the service to be monitored was not life threatening, I was asked to cancel my monitor.

Other examples of how litigation prevents both appropriate medical necessity monitoring were my experiences while the Medical Director of an HMO. When I retired from my surgical practice, I accepted the Medical Director position in a HMO. During my short tenure as the Medical Director, one of my responsibilities was to monitor the medical necessity of the services our enrollees were receiving. One of several challenges was the medical necessity of, and the charges for, a surgical procedure I had performed many times during my surgical career. The physician's response to my inquiry was a letter, and to paraphrase the letter, "If you continue with your inquiry, I will be forced to seek legal counsel to protect my physician/patient relationship." There was no question about my ability to successfully defend a lawsuit initiate by the physician, but having to pay an attorney to defend me and not be able to recover those defense costs were reasons to abandon the monitoring of the physician's services. Instead, the physician was no longer one of the HMO's providers.

The Proposed Medical Necessity Monitoring Program.

Achieving an effective and successful monitoring program for medical necessity requires the following:

1. The endorsement of the litigation reforms in Chapter 2.

2. Returning the responsibility for medical necessity monitoring to local Medical and Osteopathic Societies where the most qualified individuals to make those monitoring decisions are found, and

3. All healthcare services need to be monitored.

Each local Medical and Osteopathic Society will establish a Medical Necessity Monitoring Committee. Requests for medical necessity inquiries will be made to a Society's Committee in a different community than the one in which the physician, or other healthcare provider, being monitored practices. The Committee will appoint two physicians to a Monitoring Team, and Team's physicians will provide the same services as those to be monitored.

The Team's report will be sent to the Society's Medical Necessity Monitoring Committee. If the Team had found the service to be medically unnecessary, the Committee would offer an invitation to both the provider and patient to appear before the Committee to appeal the Committee's decision prior to any disciplinary action by the Committee.

If the provider's medical necessity appeal is lost, the provider can continue to challenge the Team's decision by requesting a Society from another community provide a Team to monitor the service. However, if the other Team finds the service to be unnecessary, the provider would have to pay the cost of the second monitor. Otherwise, appeals would become excessive.

The compensation for monitoring Team members will be established by the Provider Reimbursement Formula. [Chapter 5] The time required to make medical necessity decisions is not as much as the time required for the review of medical records and the participate in malpractice litigation.

All community providers would be obligated to accept assignments to their local Society's Monitoring Teams regardless of whether or not they were members of those Societies. Appropriate penalties will be in place for those physicians, or other healthcare providers, who refuse to accept monitoring assignments.

The proposed program for monitoring the medical necessity of all healthcare services is fair to both patients and providers. Also, the proposed monitoring program returns the control of medical necessity monitoring to local Medical and Osteopathic Societies where it once was, and where it belongs. These are compelling reasons why both the public and medical profession should endorse and adopt the program.

Achieving public and healthcare provider endorsement of the program will not be easy. Many patients are receiving, and many healthcare providers are offering, medically unnecessary services. Their legal challenges are inevitable, and both will have to rethink, or be reeducated about, their need to participate in eliminating medically unnecessary services. Healthcare's costs MUST be reduced. Their choice is either monitoring and maintaining a friendly patient and provider private healthcare delivery system or obtaining an unfriendly patient and provider National Health Service. The choice should be obvious to both!

5

Changing How Insurance Reimbursement are Calculated and Awarded

The third change to regulate the private healthcare delivery system is changing how insurance reimbursements are calculated and awarded.

Following employer's health and hospital insurance programs and after Medicare and Medicaid were introduced, billions of insurance dollars began to flow into the healthcare delivery system. But establishing the value of a service, and the amount of the reimbursement for a service, was, and has remained, a problem for both healthcare's providers and healthcare's insurers. In fact, in 2007, there is no system to establish the value of a service or the amount of its reimbursement.

Reimbursements were established initially by the insurance "game". Providers would submit every conceivable service to an insurance company, along with a charge for the service. The providers would hope the service would receive an insurance reimbursement and receive their requested service charge. Unfortunately, insurance companies denied few of those services, and they paid the requested charges unchallenged. The failure of insurance companies to challenge both the requests for insurance payments and the requested service charges resulted in many unnecessary services receiving reimbursement and many reimbursement disparities with increasing healthcare costs.

An example of the insurance game was the insurance reimbursements for hearing testing services. Prior to the 1960s, most physicians treating ear diseases and disorders performed a screening (quick) hearing test in their office. There was no charge for the test, but if a hearing loss was identified, more extensive tests were performed. At the time, the charge for the more extensive tests ranged from fifteen to twenty dollars. Those tests took about ten minutes, and patients paid for those tests from their pocketbooks. If a hearing loss was identified, and if it could not be treated medically or surgically, the patient was referred to a local businessperson called a hearing aid dealer.

During the late 1950s, physicians began to submit insurance claims for their hearing testing services along with a charge for the tests. Many insurance companies paid those claims as well as the requested charges. By the 1980s, those previously inexpensive hearing tests had increased to around $100. To support those increased reimbursements, special testing rooms were said to be required, and additional hearing tests were added. However, there were valid questions about the need for, as well as the value of, those special rooms and additional tests. But those questions were ignored. Insurance had made hearing testing a profitable service.

As could be expected, the generous reimbursements for hearing tests attracted physicians who had not previously offered office hearing testing services. To provide those services, physicians employed clinical audiologists.

During the 1970s, if generous insurance reimbursements could be obtained for testing hearing, perhaps both the testing for, and the cost of, a hearing aid could receive an insurance reimbursement. The "game" was on again.

In the early 1970s, physicians and audiologists began to lobby Congress to have Medicare pay for both testing patients for a hearing aid and for the hearing aid. In response to the lobbyists, Congress had the Food and Drug Administration investigate the hearing aid dispensing system in the United States. In 1975, I was asked to be Chairman of a Committee to conduct the investigation and to report the Committee's findings to the Food and Drug Administration.

Our Committee recommended Medicare NOT pay for the hearing aid. Unlike the ability of an examiner to establish a specific eyeglass for a specific eye refraction problem, our Committee found there were no hearing tests available to dispense a specific hearing aid for a specific hearing loss. Also, unlike testing for eyeglasses, there were no tests to determine if an individual had been dispensed the most appropriate hearing aid or if an individual was wearing the most appropriate hearing aid. If Medicare was to pay for hearing aids, the flood gates would have been opened for hearing aid dispensing abuses that could not have been proven.

Medicare did not pay for hearing aids, but Medicare did begin to pay for the hearing tests to evaluate a person for a hearing aid. The "game" had been partially successful.

The insurance reimbursements for evaluate patients for hearing aids resulted in many physicians expanding their office hearing testing services to include testing patients for, and selling, hearing aids. As the Chairman of the Committee evaluating the hearing aid dispensing system, I recommended physicians should not test for, or sell, hearing aids from their offices. First, there were no tests capable of enabling a physician to establish if their patient had received the most appropriate hearing aid. Second, few, if any, physicians were trained in how to test a patient for a hearing aid or in how to modify a hearing aid and its ear-mold to make the amplified sound more acceptable to the listener. Without adequate training in testing procedures or in hearing aids, how could physicians evaluate the quality of the services provided by their employed audiologists?

The loss of Medicare payments for hearing aids disappointed many physicians and audiologists, and the complaints and criticism I received from them seemed to never end. Although the Committee's recommendations were challenged several times, the challenges were never successful. Unfortunately, the challenges were not for the purpose of benefiting either patients or the hearing aid dispensing system. The issue was the loss of income from insurance reimbursements for hearing aids.

Another example of the insurance game was the insurance payment for a fiberoptic examination of a patient's throat and larynx (voice box) in the office. The fiberoptic instrument is inserted into the nose and passed back into the throat. A much better view of the larynx is obtained. Prior to the fiberoptic instrument, the examination was performed by passing a mirror into the back of a patient's mouth. I had been using the fiberoptic instrument in my office to replace the mirror. Since the fiberoptic examination was replacing the mirror, and since it required no additional time for the examination, I was not charging for its use.

Following a discussion of its use at a meeting, I was asked what my fee was for the procedure. I said nothing. To my surprise, I discovered several physicians were receiving insurance reimbursements of several hundred dollars each time they used the instrument during their office examination of a patient. Those physicians had submitted claims to insurance companies (the game), and their claims had been accepted and paid.

The use of the "game" to determine whether or not a service can receive an insurance reimbursement and the amount of the reimbursement is no longer acceptable. Why?

Beginning in the 1990s. Medicare and the managed healthcare industry had become major healthcare insurers, and they began to reduce the amount of their reimbursements to their healthcare providers. By 2000, those reduced reimbursement had become an economic problem for many physicians. At the same time the provider's reimbursements were being reduced, Medicare's and the managed healthcare industry's bureaucratic and other administrative costs were increasing. If Medicare's and the managed healthcare industry's increasing administrative and management costs were to be paid by arbitrarily reducing their reimbursements to their healthcare providers, a more equitable system had to be found to calculate and award those reimbursements. A standard was necessary, and the Provider Reimbursement Formula proposed in this chapter provides the standard.

The Proposed Changes in How Insurance Reimbursements are Calculated and Awarded.

The proposed changes eliminate three methods used previously to arbitrarily establish the value of, and the insurance reimbursement for, healthcare's services. In addition, the proposed changes introduce a Formula to establish those reimbursements. The Formula provides physicians the opportunity to assume a leadership role in determining the value of, and the amount of the insurance reimbursement for, their services.

The three payment methods eliminated are:

1. Stop "relative value" payments.
The relative value payment system states the more valuable a service is in diagnosing and treating a disorder or disease, the larger is its insurance reimbursement. This payment system became popular during the 1970s to justify the increasing

number of medically unnecessary services being offered patients. No service has a "relative value". A service is either necessary or it is not necessary.

2. Stop awarding insurance payments for medically unnecessary services.
Adopting the litigation recommendations in Chapter 2 will enable the medical necessity monitoring recommendations in Chapter 4 to become both active and effective. Together, both will provide physicians the opportunity to identify medically unnecessary services and eliminate their insurance reimbursements.

3. Stop reimbursement disparities.
Procedure services have been receiving the larger reimbursements. This is wrong. It takes the same amount of training, knowledge, and skill to become a physician who offers no procedure services (Internist, Family Physician, and Pediatrician) as it does to become a physician who offers procedure services (surgeon). Therefore, the reimbursements for all physician's services should be the same.

The Formula.

To provide all physicians, and other healthcare providers, appropriate reimbursements for their services, a Formula is introduced to establish the value of, and the reimbursement for, all of healthcare's services. The Formula is referred to as the Provider Reimbursement Formula, and it has three components.

1. The cost of the provider
2. The time required to complete a service.
3. The office overhead allowance.

The Cost of The Provider.

The Formula assigns an hourly payment rate for all of healthcare's providers (wage controls—Addendum I). A physician's suggested (1988) hourly pay rate is $200/hour. All rates are negotiable

Each state's Medical and Osteopathic Society will establish a method of appointing members from their local Societies to a State's reimbursement Committee. Using the Formula as their standard, the Committee will review, and will make decisions about, reimbursement policies.

The Time Required To Complete A Service.

The second component of the Provider Reimbursement Formula is the time required to complete a service. With few exceptions, the time required to complete the many different healthcare services is established and easily obtained. The Formula refers to them as the "service time", and the provider's insurance reimbursement is based on the service time.

The Office Overhead Allowance. (OOA)

The third component of the Provider Reimbursement Formula is the Office Overhead Allowance (OOA). It provides reimbursements for a provider's office expenses, and it is in addition to the provider's service time reimbursement. The OOA will vary in different regions of the country and with different specialties.

The insurance reimbursement for the OOA is calculated by considering both the time an office is available to offer patients services and the amount of money the Formula allows each specialty for their annual office expenses.

a. Office availability.
The Formula considers every office to be available to offer patient services 40hr./ week for 52 weeks each year. This amounts to 2080 hours of office availability annually.

b. Office expenses.
The amount of money the Formula allows providers for their annual office expenses will vary with the different specialties, and with the different regions in the country. Establishing the allowable amount will require consultations with the different specialty organizations, and those amounts can be established from existing office records within four to six months.
The OOA reimbursement is based on the physician's service time.

Five examples of the Provider
Reimbursement Formula.

The following five examples illustrate how easily the Formula can be applied to calculate the insurance reimbursements for physicians, and other healthcare providers.

A. The Cost of the Provider .

In all of the following five examples, each provider is a physician who receives $200/hr. for their service time. (1988) If a physician offers 1920 hours of service time each year (40hr./week for 48 weeks—four weeks away for vacation and meetings), their insurance service time reimbursements would amount to $384,000.

B. The time to Complete a Service.

The calculation of the service times is listed in each of the examples.

C. The Office Overhead Allowance. (OOA)

In each of the five examples, the OOA was calculated to be $67 for each hour of the five provider's service times, and it was calculated as follows:

1.   The office availability for each of the five providers was 40hrs./week for 52 weeks each year, or a total of 2080 hours of office availability annually.

2.   The money the Formula allowed each of the five physicians for their office expenses was $139,500. By dividing 2080 hours of office availability time into the $139,500, a $67/hr. Office Overhead Allowance was established for each hour of the physician's service time.

An OOA is included when physicians provided service outside of their office such as operations. An office must be maintained while a provider is offering services outside of their office.

Providers may spend more than the Formula's allowance for their office expenses, but their insurance reimbursement will be calculated on the Formula's OOA for their specialty.

Example One.

Example one is a surgical procedure whose present charge is $6,000. Applying the Provider Reimbursement Formula (PRF), the insurance reimbursement for this operation is:

1.   The cost of the provider:

   The provider is a physician who receives $200/hr. of service time.

2. The service time required to complete this service:

    a. The time required to complete the preoperative records and talk to patient. 15min.

    b. Time to complete the operation 3 1/2hr.

        The time to complete the operation is the time the operating room is occupied. This includes the time required to introduce the anesthesia, to prep the patient prior to the surgery, the surgery, and the time required to awaken and remove the patient from the operating room.

    c. Time to complete the post operative records 30 min.

    d. Daily post operative visits 1 1/2hrs.

        The patient's LOS (length of stay) for this operation is six days. With two daily visits, one for 10 min. and another for 5 min.. The total time is 11/2 hrs. for the six days.

    e. Time to complete discharge records 15 min.

The Formula allows a service time of 6hrs. to complete this operation. The surgeon's reimbursement is $1,200. (6 hrs X $200/hr.)

3. The Office Overhead Allowance. (OOA)

    ($67 for every hour of service time is paid for the OOA for all five physicians in these examples.)

    The OOA for this 6 hr. surgery is $402. (6 hrs. X $67/hr. of service Time.)

The Formula's reimbursement for this operation is $1,602. ($1,200 for the surgeon's service time + $402 for the surgeon's OOA).

The Formula saves $4,398 each time this operation is performed. (The present charge was $6,000, and a Formula's reimbursement is $1,602.)

Example Two.

The second example is an office procedure whose present charge is $850. Applying the Provider Reimbursement Formula (PRF), the provider's reimbursement is calculated as follows:

1. The cost of the provider:

    The provider is a physician who receives $200/hr. of service time.

In this example, in addition to the physician, an additional person is required to assist in performing the office procedure. The cost of the person, or persons, required to assist in performing office procedures is incorporated into the calculation of the office procedure's reimbursement.

2. The time required to complete the service:

    a. To review the patient/s chart and complete the necessary records 20 min.

    b. To perform the office procedure 20 min.

    c. To discuss the results with the patient and complete necessary records 20 min.

    The Formula allows one (1) hour of service time for this office procedure, and the physician's service time reimbursement is $200. ($200/hr. X 1 hr. of service time).
    The assistant's reimbursement is included in the procedure's insurance reimbursement.

3. The Office Overhead Allowance (OOA);

    The Formula's OOA for this physician is $67/hr. (1 hr. of service time X $67)

4. Office Procedure Reimbursements.

    The insurance reimbursements for office procedures, special treatments, and studies are calculated by considering the initial cost of any equipment, medications, etc. required to offer the procedure, special treatments, or studies; by the depreciation and maintenance costs; and by the cost of the personnel required to assist in offering the service. The space (room) for the procedure is included in the physician's office space requirements.

    The Insurance Reimbursement for the office procedure in this example is $55 each time the procedure is performed. ($25 for the equipment's cost, depreciation, and maintenance, plus $30/hr. for the personnel required to assist in the procedure.)

If a physician's presence is not needed during an office procedure, the procedure's insurance reimbursement will not include a reimbursement for the physician. However, the procedure's reimbursement will include a reimbursement for the physician's time to interpret the result of the procedure at a later time. Most of the service times for interpreting office procedures would be five minutes, and the reimbursement would be $17 ($200/hr. of service time divided by 12 = $17. There are 12 five minute segments in one hour.)

The total insurance reimbursement for this office procedure is $322. The physician's service time is $200. (A physician was required to be present during the procedure.) The physician's OOA is $67, and the procedure's reimbursement is $55. Since the physician was present during the procedure, no physician reimbursement is offered for interpreting the procedure's results.)

Each time this procedure is performed, the Formula saves $528. (The Present charge is $850, and the Formula's reimbursement is $322)

Example Three.

The present charge for this procedure is about $800. Applying the Formula to calculate its insurance reimbursement:

1. The cost of the provider.

    The provider is a physician who receives $200/hr. of service time.

2. The time to complete the service:

    a. To complete the patient's preoperative records and prepare the patient for the operation 15 min.

    b. To complete the procedure 20 min.

    c. To give the patient their postoperative instructions and complete their records 15 min.

    The Formula allows 50 minutes for this procedure, and the physician's service time reimbursement is $167. (50 min. at $200/hr. = $167)

3.   The Office Overhead Allowance.

The OOA for this procedure is $56. (5O min. of $67/hr. = $56)

The total reimbursement for this procedure is $223. (The service time reimbursement is $167, and the OOA is $56.)

The Formula saves $577 each time this procedure is performed.

Example Four

The fourth example of the Provider Reimbursement Formula is the calculation of the reimbursements for office visits. Different specialties will have different office visit requirements, such as:

1. The time a physician needs to spend with each patient.
In most instances, three different times are required—a quick five minutes office visit to determine if the patient is progressing satisfactorily, a fifteen minutes office visit, and a thirty minutes office visit for new patients.

The specialty example used for this discussion is specialty XYZ, and it has a five minutes office visit, a fifteen minutes office visit, and a thirty minutes office visit with insurance code numbers for each of the three office visit.

Although physicians may be with their patients only a few minutes, additional time is required for patients to receive additional services from the physician's support personnel. For example, a support person may be reviewing a patient's history and medications, or may be performing a superficial examination prior to the physician entering the room. In addition, the support person may assist the physician by writing notes in the patient's chart during the physician's examination and will frequently provide patients their instructions about medications, treatment program, etc. after the physician leaves the room.

2. The cost of, the number of, and type of, office personnel required to provide patients their office services.

In our example, specialty XYZ requires a secretary, a receptionist, and one nurse. Other specialties may require technicians, physician assistants, and other personnel.

When more than one physician practices in the same office, one physician will receive the Formula's full support personnel allowance, and each of the other physicians will receive one half of the allowance. All percentages are negotiable. For example, the Formula allows specialty XYZ $100,000 annually for its required office personnel. One physician will receive the full $100,000, and each of the other physicians will receive 50%, or $50,000, for their personnel allowance.

3. The office space requirements.
Again, when establishing space allowances for groups of physicians, one physician in the group will receive the full space allowance, and each of the other physicians in the group will receive 50% of the space allowance.

In our example, the Formula allows specialty XYZ 2000 square feet for its space allowance, and allows $20,000 for its annual cost. Each additional physician in the group will be allowed 1000 square feet of additional office space and $10,000 for its cost.

4. The cost of the office equipment and the cost of the disposables.
Different specialties will have the need for different office equipment such as desks, chairs, tables, computers, Fax machines, copiers, examination tables, instruments, cabinets, etc.. This type of equipment is purchased one time, and it has a depreciation allowance.

The office disposables are medications, office insurances, telephones, paper materials, mailings, maintenance, etc. required to both treat patients and operate an office.

The Formula's allowance for the office equipment is based on the equipment's annual depreciation allowance. The allowance for the office disposable items is their full value. In this example, specialty XYZ's initial purchase price for its office equipment was $200,000. The annual depreciation allowance for the equipment is $15,000. The Formula allows $5,000 annually for the disposables required to treat patients and operate the office. The Formula's allowance for specialty XYZ's office equipment and its disposables, is $20,000 annually.

When there is a group of physicians practicing in one office, and all physicians are using the same office equipment as required for the one physician, only one physician will receive the office equipment depreciation allowance. The other physicians would receive no office equipment depreciation allowance, but they would receive 50% of the disposables allowance.

The existing IRS rules for corporations, etc. require an accounting person with more knowledge than I possess to establish the accounting rules regarding the Formula's Office Overhead Allowances (OOA).

5. The malpractice insurance costs.
The cost of a physician's malpractice insurance for specialty XYZ is $60,000, and each physician in a group will receive the FULL malpractice insurance allowance.

All of the information regarding the office visit service times, office personnel, office space, office equipment depreciation, office disposables, and malpractice insurance is easily obtained from existing office records.

The following examples are the calculation of the office visit reimbursements for specialty XYZ located in a particular region of the country.

1. The specialty requires a five minutes, a ten minutes, and a thirty minutes office visit. (The time the physician spends with the patient.)

2. The support personnel required to assist one physician is a receptionist, a secretary, and one nurse, and the Formula allows $100,000 for the cost of their annual salaries and benefits.

3. The space requirement for one physician for this specialty is 2000 square feet, and the Formula allows $20,000 for the annual cost of the space in the physician's region of the country.

4. The annual office equipment depreciation allowance for specialty XYZ is $15,000, and the disposable's allowance is $5,000 for a total allowance of $20,000.

5. The malpractice insurance allowance for each physician in specialty XYZ is $60,000.

For one physician, the Formula allows a $200,000 total Office Overhead Allowance for specialty XYZ. ($100,000 for personnel, $20,000 for space, $15,000 for the office equipment depreciation, $5,000 for the disposables, and $60,000 for malpractice insurance).

If there is more than one physician in the same office, each of the other physicians will receive 100% of their malpractice insurance and 50% of the $100,000 personnel, $20,000 space, and $5,000 disposables allowances.

Applying the Provider Reimbursement Formula to calculate the insurance reimbursements for the office visits for one physician in specialty XYZ:

A. The cost of the provider.
The provider is physician who receives $200 for each hour of service time.

B. The time to complete the service:
    a. A five minutes office visit.
    b. A fifteen minutes office visit.
    c. A thirty minutes office visit.

C. The Office Overhead Allowance. (OOA).
For one physicians, the Formula allows a total office expense of $200,000 for personnel, space, office equipment allowances, disposables, and malpractice insurance.

To calculate the OOA/hr. of a physician's service time, the office is available 40 hr. each week for 52 weeks/year for a total of 2080 hours. (Although the physician may be in the office only 48 weeks, the office and its personnel are available during the time the physician is away.) By dividing 2080 hours into the $200,000 allowed office expenses, each hour of office availability costs $96/hr.. Or, there is an OOA of $96 for each hour of one physician's service time.

Using the Formula to calculate the office visit reimbursements for one physician in specialty XYZ:

a. The reimbursement for a five minutes office visit is:

1. The cost of the provider.

    The provider is a physician who receives $200/hour for their service time.

2. The time required to complete the service:

    The service time is 5 minutes. There are 12 5 minutes segments in each hour. By dividing 12 into $200, each 5 minutes office visit receives a $17 physician service time reimbursement.

3. The Office Overhead Allowance. (OOA)

    The Formula allows an OOA of $96 for each hour a physician's service time. For each 5 minutes office visit, the OOA is $8. (Divide 12 into $96/hr.)

The reimbursement for a 5 minutes office visit for spcialty XYZ for one physician is $25. ($17 is for the physician's service time + $8for the OOA.)

The reimbursement for a fifteen minutes office visit for one physician in specialty XYZ is $74. ($50 is for the physician's service time + $24 is for the OOA.)

The reimbursement for a thirty minutes office visit for one physician is $148. ($100 is for the physician's service time + $48 is for OOA.)

The office visit reimbursements for each of the other physicians in the same office are calculated and awarded the same as for the one physician's office visit except the Formula's OOA for each of the other physicians will be only 50% of the personnel, space, and disposables allowances.

There are times the physician does not provide the patient their services during an office visit. Instead, the physician's support personnel provide those services. When the physician does not examine or treat the patient during an office visit, there is no physician service time calculated into the Formula's office visit reimbursement for that patient. Instead, the Formula's reimbursement for the patient would be the physician's OOA for that specialty. For example, for specialty XYZ, the reimbursement for a patient's fifteen minutes office visit without a physician would be the specialty's OOA of $24.

Monitoring the medical necessity of office visits is easily accomplished with existing code numbers and computers. For example, a possible insurance misusage would be a physician requesting insurance reimbursements for six hours of physician service time. But only eight patients had office visits that day, and none of those patients were new patients. Another example of possible insurance misuse would be a patient having four consecutive office visits lasting fifteen minutes for disease "A" when the standard of care for the treatment of the disease is only one fifteen minutes initial office visit followed by two five minutes office visit.

Example Five.

The fifth example of the Provider Reimbursement Formula is the calculation of the insurance reimbursements for initial hospital consultations and for the physician's visits following the initial consultation. Many of those consultations and post-consultation visits are medically unnecessary. However, until malpractice reforms (Chapter 2) are adopted, the threat of litigation forces physicians to request more hospital consultations than are necessary to protect themselves from lawsuits.

The Provider Reimbursement Formula offers three types of physician reimbursements for hospital consultations. In all of the following examples, the consultants are physicians who receive $200/hr. for their service time, and each physician's OOA is $73/hr. for each hour of service time.

1. For an initial consultation, the Formula allows thirty minutes and offers a $137.00 reimbursement. ($100 for the physician's 30 minutes service time and $37 for the OOA.

2. For the first visit following the initial consultation, the Formula allows a fifteen minutes visit and offers a $68 reimbursement. ($50 for the physician's service time + $18 for the physician's OOA).

3. The Formula allows a five minutes visit for each additional hospital visit, and it offers a $23 reimbursement. ($17 for the physician's service time + $6 for the OOA)

Although physicians may be with their hospitalized patients only a few minutes, they require additional time to review the patient's hospital chart and record appropriate notes in the chart. The number of visit following the initial consultation would be closely monitored.

Other applications of the Formula.

No examples are presented of how the Provider Reimbursement Formula calculates the reimbursements for X rays, laboratory, and other diagnostic studies. However, the Formula does establish their reimbursements and provides significant savings.

The Formula and Wage Controls.

The Provider Reimbursement Formula introduces wage and price controls, and they are discussed in Addendum I.

The Formula and the Indemnity Insurance industry.

The Formula can provide additional healthcare dollars to purchase patient services by replacing the existing managed healthcare industry's expensive management bureaucracies and infrastructure operating costs with the indemnity insurance industry's less expensive management and operating costs. (Addendum V)

The Formula and the Business Community.

Along with the Formula's significant reductions in healthcare's costs, the Formula will stabilize healthcare's costs. (Wage and price controls—Addendum I) Business will benefit from the stabilization.

Hopefully, the Formula will become the standard to establish the value of, and the reimbursements for, all of healthcare's services.

6

Co-payments

Co-payments are the fourth change to regulate a private healthcare delivery system

Some type of health insurance, and not the patient's pocketbook, will continue to be the primary source of payment for healthcare's services. Therefore, patients will continue to think of their services as "free". The need to have patients consider the cost of those "free" services, requires the introduction of co-payments.

All of healthcare's services require co-payments, and the amount of those co-payments are negotiable. However, those co-payments must be large enough to force patients to consider the necessity of, as well as the cost of, their services.

Co-payment adjustments may be necessary for both Medicaid and some Medicare patients, but their services would be closely monitored for their medical necessity.

Patients will pay their co-payment directly to their healthcare provider, and the provider will deducted those co-payments from their request for insurance reimbursements.

7

Reducing Hospital Costs

The fifth change to regulate the existing private healthcare delivery system is the regulation of a hospital's allowable fixed costs and the monitoring of its variable costs.

Prior to the 1960s, most patients paid for their hospital services from their pocketbooks, and those patients unable to pay for their services were able to obtain free services in city, county, and community hospitals. But beginning in the 1950s, employer's hospital insurance, and in the late 1960s, Medicare's and Medicaid's hospital insurance, provided most patients the opportunity to have their hospitalizations paid by their insurance. Unfortunately, those insurance programs were not monitor either the medical necessity of their policyholder's hospital admissions, the need for the hospital days following the admissions, or the hospital's increasing service charges. Those monitoring failures allowed hospital costs to increase far more rapidly than the rate of inflation, and hospitals became profitable. Those profits were attracting businesspersons and their investors, and in the mid 1970s, the managed healthcare legislation offered them the opportunity to enter into, and later control, hospital management. Hospitals rapidly became for-profit multi-hospital business systems rather than the tradirtional nonprofit and charitable community hospital system.

Hospital costs can be reduced by at least 30%, and more, by regulating a hospital's allowable fixed costs and by monitoring its variable costs.

Fixed Costs.

Fixed costs are always present regardless of the number of patients in the hospital. Reductions in those fixed costs can be achieved by regulating the services allowed to be considered fixed costs and the amount of money a hospital can apply to each patient's daily charges for those services.

The following examples are some of the fixed costs that can be either reduced or eliminated.

Hospital Construction costs.

Hospitals construction needs to focus on patient service requirements rather than on aesthetics. When one enters a hospital, they are not entering a luxury hotel. Achieving appropriate treatment is the goal, and aesthetics, and the availability of medically unnecessary services and conveniences, should not be a consideration.

Hospital construction costs began to increase after World War II. Following that war, many of the taxes to support the war were never cancelled. Those taxes provided government much money to spend on social programs. One of those social programs was legislation offering money to communities to build hospitals. Beginning in the 1950s, and accelerating during the 1960s, the money from government grants and from hospital insurance programs was providing communities the money to build hospitals. Unfortunately, too many of those hospitals were constructed for the community's pride rather than for its medical needs.

Unnecessary construction costs are rooms with two beds. Those rooms began to appear during the late 1960s. Prior to the 1960s, most hospitals had rooms with four to six beds for semiprivate patients, and ten or more beds for charity patients. Rooms with only two beds have increased construction costs. They require additional walls to separate the rooms and long corridors to gain access to the rooms. Future hospital construction should require hospitals to construct the less expensive to build and maintain rooms with four to six beds.

In addition to their increased construction and maintenance costs, rooms with only two beds isolate patients. Nurses must walk up and down long corridors to attend their patients, and the communication between nurse and patient is through a public address system. Observe the more effective nursing care offered patients in multi-bed intensive care areas.

My preference for hospital construction has always been a central core containing the nurse's station surrounded by several rooms with four to six beds and glass walls facing the nursing station. This configuration provides nurses the ability to monitor and serve their patients more effectively. Furthermore, the configuration requires less square footage and construction costs than do the existing rooms with two beds.

There will always be the need for private rooms for those patients with illnesses or other circumstances requiring isolation, but their indiscriminate use must be discouraged.

Specialty Hospitals.

Another unnecessary hospital fixed cost is the need for all hospitals in the same community to offer the same services. Instead, some hospital services need to be restricted to one hospital. The cost of providing every hospital the equipment and the trained personnel required to provide the same service in every hospital increases the cost of providing the service in each hospital. In addition, both the quality and the medical necessity of the service provided by specialty hospitals can be more effectively monitored.

Not every community requires a special hospital for every service. Identifying those communities or regions where specialty hospitals would be cost effective can be easily accomplished. Physicians should participate in making those determinations.

Present transporting opportunities provide patients safe and rapid transportation from one hospital to another.

For-profit Hospital Management Companies.

Both entrepreneurs within the business community and a free market economy are to be encouraged. Both have made our country the great nation it has become, and it has rewarded those who have initiated innovative programs and products. However, profiting from a patient's need for hospitalization is not acceptable. Medicine is not part of the free market economy. (Addendum I) Patients do not have the choice of deciding whether or not they want to be hospitalized. Therefore, hospitals should remain charitable community institutions rather than the for-profit businesses they have become.

Why healthcare is not a business is discussed in Addendum II

Hospital Management Costs.

An increasing hospital fixed cost is the cost of hospital management. Much of the increasing cost has been the need to employ more management personnel to comply with the many hospital regulations and documentation requirements. But, the cost of the salaries and benefits offered to some management personnel have become excessive.

Managing a hospital is entirely different than managing a business. A hospital would continue to function if its management had made bad decisions; however, a business could be lost if its management had made bad decisions. Therefore, comparing hospital management's salaries, responsibilities, and benefits with those in the business community is not realistic.

Hospitals can function effectively and efficiently without the excessive salaries and benefits offered to some management personnel. Furthermore, the proposed Provider Reimbursement Formula offers physicians $200/hr. There is no reason why hospital management should receive more.

While the member of a hospital's Board of Trustees, I disagreed frequently with members of the Board representing the business community during budget discussions. They were unable to understand why I questioned the disparity between some management salaries and benefits with those offered to our nurses. Where were the hospital's priorities? The hospital could function with a management staff receiving smaller salaries and benefits, but the hospital could not function without nurses. Why not give the nurses the salaries, bonuses, cars, country club dues, etc. given to some in management?

Hospital Regulations.

Unnecessary regulations and documentation requirements have created significant and unnecessary fixed costs for hospitals. Many of those regulations were required to respond to litigation pressures. However, others have been created to perpetuate the healthcare bureaucracies. Those regulations need to be reviewed for their medical necessity by the healthcare providers required to respond to them. Also, adopting the litigation reforms in Chapter 2 will eliminate many of those regulations and documentation requirements.

The Cost of Hospital Litigation.

Lawsuits have created a significant fixed cost for all hospitals, and at least 60% of those litigation costs could be eliminated by endorsing the litigation reforms proposed in Chapter 2.

Hospital Education Programs.

Those education programs funded by a hospitalized patient's insurance need to be reviewed, and some eliminated. One example of an expensive education program that needs to be reviewed is the cost of a hospital's resident physician training program. A resident physician is a student. Should a patient's hospital insurance be subsidizing their education?

Prior to the 1970s, a resident physician's salary could be justified. Hospitals had outpatient clinics and multi-bed inpatient wards providing free care to charity patients. Those patients received their medical and surgical services from the hospital's resident physicians, and the resident physician's services were supervised by the hospital's Medical Staff members. The resident physician's received a salary for providing those services, and the salary averaged $50 to $75 a month. Laundry, room, and board were included. But during the 1960s, the money hospitals began to receive from unregulated hospital insurance offered them the opportunity to increase their resident physician's salaries. By 2005, those salaries had increased to as much as $35,000, and hospitalized patient's insurance was paying those salaries.

Since hospitals no longer have free outpatient clinics and inpatient wards, they no longer need to pay their resident physicians. Now, instead of learning their clinical skills by examining and treating the patients in the hospital's free outpatient clinics and inpatient wards, resident physicians learn their clinical skills by examining and treating the Medical Staff's private patients.

If hospitals were to establish the free outpatient clinics and inpatient hospital wards recommended and discussed in the next chapter, resident physicians would be providing most of those free services, and hospitals would have a reason to provide their resident physicians salaries. Also, those salaries could become an acceptable hospital fixed cost paid by hospitalized patient's insurance. But, using the $75 per month in the 1950s as the standard, an appropriate inflationary index would be used to establish their salaries in 2007.

Articles have been written recommending hospitals pay their resident physicians larger salaries to attract them to the hospital's area with the hope those residents would remain in the area and practice medicine following their training. This policy is not realistic. Most physicians select a training program for its training opportunities rather than for either its salary or location. Most resident physicians leave the area after their hospital training to practice their profession in another location. Also, hospitals providing better training opportunities are able to offer smaller salaries and attract better physicians to their residency training programs.

Hospital Marketing Programs.

Marketing programs are another unnecessary hospital fixed cost, and they need to be eliminated. During the 1950s and 1960s, communities were constructing hospitals with too many beds; however, those hospitals were able to occupy those beds with patients who did not require hospitalization. I can remember patients being admitted for their annual physical examinations. But, during the 1970s, as Medicare's hospital costs increased, Medicare initiated monitoring programs to establish the medical necessity of Medicare hospital admissions. Many unnecessary admissions were identified as well as many unnecessary hospital days following the admissions. Eliminating those unnecessary Medicare admissions and the hospital days following the admissions created many empty beds in most hospitals. To attract patients to occupy those beds, hospitals initiated expensive marketing programs. Those marketing expenses should not be allowed as a hospital's fixed cost. A hospital's image should be created by the excellence of its services rather than by its marketing program. Hospitals are not businesses. Hospitals have only one purpose—to provide patients their necessary healthcare services.

Providing patients pamphlets with instructions regarding a service is not a marketing program.

Hospital Variable Costs.

Variable costs are those costs created when services are provided hospitalized patients, and those costs will vary with the number of patients in the hospital and with the cost of the services provided those patients. Variable costs can be reduced by:

1. An accounting system to record the cost of the services offered to each hospitalized patient.

2. A penalty for those medical staff members who provide their patients unnecessary services, and

3. Litigation reforms.

Recording the Cost of Patient's Services.

One method of recording both the services patients receive and their costs is the DRG. DRG is an acronym for Diagnostic Related Groups.

When Medicare was introduced in the late 1960s, hospitals were unable to provide Medicare information about their costs for providing patients different services. To acquire that information, Medicare funded the faculty at Yale University to developed an accounting system, and it was called the DRGs. The system classifies all diseases, disorders, and procedures into 473 DRGs. When Medicare patients were discharged from hospitals, their disorder, disease, or procedure was assigned a DRG. All of the services a patient received during their hospitalization, as well the cost of those services, were recorded in the patient's DRG.

DRGs offer hospitals the following information about their variable costs.

1. DRGs can identify the cost of treating different diseases and disorders.

2. DRGs can compare the cost of treating the same disease and disorder in each community and regional hospital.

3. DRGs can provide hospitals the information necessary to compare the cost of the services offered by different Medical Staff members treating the same diseases and disorders, and

4. DRGs make each Medical Staff member accountable for the cost of the services they offer their patients.

Penalties for Unnecessary Services.

In addition to a DRG accounting system, variable costs can be reduced by having an expensive penalty for those staff members offering unnecessary services. My suggestion had been a bed tax. When a physician admits a patient to the hospital, the physician is "taxed" an amount of money each day their patient is hospitalized. If the cost of the services offered the patient during their hospitalization is equal to, or less than, the average regional DRG cost for treating the same disease or disorder, the physician would not have to pay the "tax" for that patient. The bed tax would have to be large enough to have Medical Staff members consider seriously the medical necessity of the services they offer their patients.

There may be circumstances requiring the cost of the services required to treat a patient's disease or disorder greater than the region's average DRG cost. However, the medical necessity of those services would be evaluated following the patient's discharge.

Hospital Litigation.

Once again, litigation surfaces its ugly head. By reducing the need for physicians to provide their patients unnecessary services, a hospital's variable costs could be reduced significantly. But physicians cannot be expected to order only medically necessary services if they are not provided protection from frivolous malpractice lawsuits

The Quality of Care in Hospitals.

The quality of the care provided hospitalized patients and the unnecessary deaths resulting from those quality issues appear to have become popular topics in recent publications. One such article was "Fixing Hospitals. Medical Errors Kill 100,000 Americans Every Year", in Forbes magazine, June 2005 issue.

Most of the articles discussing quality of care issues have expressed the usual bureaucratic response: "the need to improve hospital quality control systems". But, if the authors of those articles had know the practice of medicine prior to the 1970s, they would realize the present quality of care issues in hospitals are not "the need to improve hospital quality control system". Those quality problems are the result of both the discipline and training issues that have become a problem among both some physicians and nurses. Discipline became a problem following the cultural changes that occurred during the 1960s, and training deficiencies became a problem following the closure of the free clinics that had provided the patient resource for training both physicians and nurses. (Addendum IV)

An example of both a discipline and training problem was a recent experience a patient had with a breathing problem following thyroid surgery. The nurse notified the resident physician the patient was having a breathing problem, but neither the resident physician nor the nurse appreciated the seriousness of a breathing problem following thyroid surgery. Since the nurse did not sound concerned, the resident physician neither examined the patient nor called the operating surgeon.

To obtain the appropriate care, the family member called their son who is a physician in another community. His son called the operating surgeon at his home, and the surgeon returned to the hospital immediately. Emergency surgery was preformed.

Discipline issue: Thirty years ago, following a review of such an incident, the resident physician would have been dismissed. But, in 2006, probably nothing was done to avoid the expense of defending a lawsuit initiated by the resident physician following their dismissal. Training issue: Breathing problems following thyroid surgery are life threatening. Why was a nurse with no knowledge of breathing problems following surgery allowed to be responsible for this patient's post operative care?

Summary.

Opposition to the proposed restructuring of a hospital's allowable fixed costs can be expected from both the investor owned and profit driven multi-hospital management companies and from physicians and other healthcare providers who own healthcare facilities, such as Outpatient Surgical Centers and Rehabilitation Centers.

Variable costs can be reduced by adopting the recommendations proposed in this chapter. But implementing those recommendations and achieving those reductions will not be possible without litigation reform. (Chapter 2)

Although hospital quality of care issues are real issues, the solution is not "improving quality control systems". The solution is recognizing and addressing the discipline and training problems that have evolved since the 1970s among many physicians and nurses.

8

Establishing Free Outpatient and Inpatient Healthcare Facilities

The sixth change to regulate the private healthcare delivery system is establishing free outpatient and inpatient healthcare facilities like those that existed prior to the 1970s.

Before the introduction of health and hospital insurance, large city and county hospitals, as well as most community hospitals, offered free healthcare services in outpatient clinics and inpatient hospital wards. Most of the physicians providing those free services in the city and county hospitals were salaried physicians employed by medical schools. Their compensation was necessary to provide those physicians an income for their services to those free patients as they taught medical students and resident physicians medicine and surgery. The free services patients received in community hospitals were provided by the hospital's Medical Staff. In addition to those Medical Staff members, other community physicians volunteered their services. Prior to health insurance, physicians entering the practice of medicine required several years to develop a private practice with enough private patients capable of paying their service charges. Volunteering their services in those free healthcare facilities offered those physicians the opportunity to maintain their clinical skills while their private practice developed. Also, physician's offered free services in offices. The gifts my wife and I received from patients who received my free services were special.

By the early 1970s, the number of patients with insurance had reduced the need for those free facilities, and they closed. Unfortunately, along with their closure, insurance had conjured the idea among many physicians they no longer had to offer their services without payment. Both the closure of the free facilities and the refusal of physicians to offer their services without payment caused an increasing number of patients to have difficulty obtaining their healthcare services.

Although most individuals will continue to have health and hospital insurance, there will always be individuals without either insurance or the ability to pay for their services. Therefore, our country's future healthcare delivery system must provide facilities offering free services. But instead of the large city and county hospitals with hundreds of beds like those existing prior to the 1970s, the proposed free outpatient and inpatient facilities would be established in local community hospitals. Many of those free facilities in community hospitals would be associated with medical schools. Since the closing of the large city and county hospitals, medical schools have had to affiliate with community hospitals to obtain enough patients for their students and resident physicians to examine and treat.

Placing the free facilities in existing community hospitals would not be a problem. Patients are already seeking free services in their emergency rooms, and the proposed free outpatient clinics would be located in those emergency rooms. Salaried fulltime primary care physicians would be employed to staff those free outpatient clinics, and the free inpatient services would be provided by the hospital's Medical Staff. As discussed previously, hospitals offer their Medical Staff members special income generating opportunities. They can admit their patients to the hospital and use the hospital's equipment, personnel, and other resources at no cost to themselves. In return for the use of those resources, Medical Staff members had been required to offer their services to patients in the hospital's free outpatient clinics and inpatient wards without compensation. The practice should be reinstated

A compelling reason for physicians to support and staff the proposed free facilities in their community hospitals would be to deter government's intrusion into, and its ultimate control of, healthcare. Those facilities, rather than government, would be providing the necessary healthcare services to patients unable to purchase their services.

In addition to the hospital's employed and salaried fulltime primary care physician staffing the hospital's free outpatient clinic facilities, other community physicians will seek the opportunity to participate in those outpatient clinics. Although insurance has enabled physicians to develop a private practice more rapidly than before insurance, the opportunity to treat patients with diseases and disorders a physician may not encounter in their private practice would attract many community physicians to obtain the opportunity to participate in their community hospital's free outpatient clinics.

Another expensive government bureaucracy is not required to administer and fund those free facilities. Several funding options are available. The space, the fulltime physician, the nursing staff, and the other administrative expenses could become an allowable hospital fixed cost. When the adoption of the six changes reduce existing hospital costs by 35% or more, the cost of the hospital's free facilities would not increase the cost of hospitalization. Other funding sources could be from private endowments, from foundations, and from local businesses as it was prior to the 1970s.

Many communities have existing tax supported free outpatient facilities as part of their Departments of Health. However, government support for the proposed free community hospital facilities should be discouraged. Government intrusion is always followed by the creation of expensive and inefficient government bureaucracies.

9

Why Support a Private Healthcare Delivery System?

In addition to the ability of a regulated private healthcare delivery system to offer quality and easily available healthcare services more comprehensively and less expensively than any other delivery system, there are two additional reasons the public should support a regulated private healthcare delivery system. One is the inability of our country's economy to support a government sponsored National Health Service, and the other is the career incentives offered by a private healthcare delivery system.

The Economy

Over the past five decades, legislators have been increasing the cost of government by increasing the size of government's bureaucratic infrastructure to administer its social program. In the 1930s, the cost of government consumed only about 4% of the country's GNP, but at this time, the cost of government consumes about 24% of our country's GNP. Also, during the past 40 years, the cost of government has been increasing faster than the economy that supports it. Budget deficits have resulted, and it is not realistic to think our country's economy can support the additional cost of a National Health Service without incurring additional deficits?

My college economics course taught me the public's ability to spend provides the strength that drives of a country's economy. When the public has money to spend, they buy "things". Their purchases generate sales taxes. In addition, the public's purchases force manufacturers to produce more "things". Producing more "things" increases business profits, and those profits increase government's business tax revenues. Furthermore, producing more "things" requires manufacturers to employ more people. Those additional employees pay income taxes, and their additional purchases generate sales taxes. Unfortunately, the country's polit-ically driven major media outlets have not discussed the enormous gain in our government's tax revenues following the tax cuts in 2002 that gave people more money to spend.

In contrast, when taxes are increased, the public has less money to spend, and they stop purchasing "things". As fewer "things" are purchased, sales tax revenues are reduced, and manufacturers are forced to reduce both their production and the number of their employees. When taxes are increased, government loses income taxes, sales taxes, and business taxes, and both recessions and unemploy-ment follow.

Why is this fundamental economic principle so difficult for so many people to understand. During the 1990s, our country had the largest state tax increases in its history, and in 1994, Congress increased federal income and other taxes. Although those state and federal taxes provided legislators billions of additional dollars to "buy" future votes, removing those dollars from the public's pockets reduced their purchasing power. Their reduced purchasing power contributed to the economic decline and unemployment that began in 1998.

Again, how much tax money can be removed from our economy to support unnecessary, but politically popular, social programs before the economy col-lapses? Or will removing more money from the public's pockets to pay the increased taxes required to support a National Health Service further reduce the public's purchasing power and initiate a significant economic recession in the United States? Economists who are not politically dependent say yes. And, who is hurt? The public! They would have increased taxes; there would be fewer jobs available; they would be dissatisfied with the curtailed services offered by a National Health Service; and the country's debt would increase.

If one thinks in terms of conspiracies, are some members in Congress seeking a National Health Service to create the need for additional taxes knowing those increased taxes would be followed by an economic slowdown with increased unemployment? Both recessions and unemployment increase public dependency on government, and increased public dependency is the goal of an increasing number of Socialists and Leftists in our government. A conspiracy?

The taxing power of our government was intended to enable it to fund the country's defense and to fund the building and maintenance of its infrastructure. However, government's major expense has become the cost of the many social and other entitlement programs politicians have introduced over the past five decades. A National Health Service should not become another one of those expensive programs. To paraphrase what someone said, "A democracy will no longer exist after its voters discover that they can vote themselves largesse (generous gifts) from the public treasury."

Career Incentives

The second reason the public should support a private healthcare delivery system is the career incentives offered by the delivery system. Career incentives are necessary to attract the best of our youth to consider becoming physicians. A reminder: there is a difference between being OFFERED services and being PROVIDED services. Both a National Health Service and HMOs can provide delivery systems OFFERING the public their healthcare services, but only physicians can PROVIDE those services. Once again: the quality of your healthcare services will depend on the abilities of the physicians providing them, and the availability of those services will depend on the number of physicians available to provide them. Without career incentives, neither the best of our youth nor than adequate number of our youth will be attracted to become physicians.

The public needs to consider the many problems associated with the time required to recover from a physician shortage. First, incentives would have to be introduced to attract the best of our youth to reconsider becoming a physician. Those incentives may require three or more years to attract those youths. After deciding to become physicians, those youths would require at least ten to twelve more years to prepare themselves to become practicing physicians. Recovering from a physicians shortage would require at least 15 years. (Chapter 11)

The ability of any "system" to attract the best individuals to the "system" is the career incentives offered by the "system". Over several decades, neither government (Medicare) nor the managed healthcare industry (HMOs) has provided those career incentives. However, a regulated private healthcare delivery system, like the one proposed in this book, has offered, and possesses the ability to continue to offer, those incentives. They are:

1. The opportunity to be independent practitioners in a fee-for-service private healthcare delivery system rather than employees in either a National Health Service or a managed healthcare company.

2. The opportunity to receive reimbursements for their services established by a standard (Provider Reimbursement Formula) rather than arbitrarily established by the insurer.

3. The opportunity to have 90% of healthcare's dollars purchasing services for patients (the private indemnity insurance industry) rather than half, or more, of those dollars supporting the bureaucracies administering a National Health Service and the managed healthcare industry.

4. The opportunity to treat patients who have had the freedom to select the providers of their choice.

5. The opportunity to determine their patient's needs independent of a third party's approval prior to the patient receiving them.

6. The opportunity to have the medical necessity of their services judged by peers who are qualified to make those judgments.

7. The opportunity to offer their patients more comprehensive, better quality, and more easily available services, at a lower cost than those offered by either an HMO or a National Health Service.

The public will not benefit from another expensive and unnecessary government social program (National Health Service). It could not provide the career incentives necessary to attract the best of our youth to become physicians. Instead, the public would benefit more from a regulated private healthcare delivery system. It possesses the career incentives necessary to attract the best of our youth to become physicians.

Both the inability of our economy to support a National Health Service and the inability of a National Health Service to attract the best of our youth to become our future physicians are two important reasons why the public not should support a National Health Service. Instead, the public needs to support a regulated private healthcare delivery system like the one proposed in this book.

10

A Message For Legislators

When both physicians and the public decide that preserving a regulated private healthcare delivery system is important, their message to their legislators needs to be:

1. Our country's existing private healthcare delivery system has provided quality healthcare services more comprehensively and more easily available than any other healthcare delivery system in the world, and

2. The existing private healthcare delivery system has only one problem. It is the unconscionable cost of its services.

3. Those costs have only one cause. It is the patient's, the physician's, and the other healthcare provider's misusages of unregulated health and hospital insurance.

4. Those insurance misusages are easily corrected by six changes that regulate healthcare's service cost and utilization in the existing private healthcare delivery system.

5. Those six changes will reduce healthcare's costs to an internationally competitive 8% to 9% of our country's GNP, and they will provide healthcare facilities offering free healthcare services to those patients unable to pay for them.

6. The cost of the healthcare bureaucracies required to administer both a National Health Service and the managed healthcare industry prevents both from achieving the reductions in healthcare's costs that are possible with a regulate private healthcare delivery system.

7. The healthcare dollars required to support those bureaucracies would reduce the number of healthcare's dollars available to purchase services for patients, and the loss of those dollars would require patient services to be curtailed.

9. Neither a National Health Service nor the managed healthcare industry can offer the career incentives necessary to attract the best of our youth to become our future physicians.

10. A healthcare delivery system has a payment system, a delivery system, and a provider system. Healthcare's services are paid by the payment system, offered by the delivery system, and provided by the provider system. The quality, the comprehensiveness, and the availability of a delivery system's healthcare services depends on the provider system. For the provider system to provide those services, it must be able to attract the best of a country's youth to become the provider system's providers. This requires the delivery system of offer the career incentives necessary to attract those providers to the provider system. The delivery system offering the best opportunity to provide those career incentives is a regulated private healthcare delivery system.

As the public ponders their need to challenge those legislators seeking to replace the private healthcare delivery system, their challenges need to focus on the following questions and answers:

1. Do I want to allow government to do to the healthcare delivery system what it has done to the education system in the United States? We have the most expensive and the worst education system in the industrialized world.

2. Can government provide my healthcare services? No. It can only sponsor a delivery system OFFERING those services. Only physicians can PROVIDE healthcare's services.

3. Can a government sponsored healthcare delivery system attract the best of our youth to be come our future physicians? No. Why not? If you possessed the ability to choose any career of your choice, would you want to spend ten to twelve years studying to become a physician whose future is a salaried employee of, and subject to the whims of, a politically driven and bureaucratically administered government agency? I don't think so.

4. Yes, there are inherent dangers in allowing a government sponsored National Health Service and the managed healthcare industry to replace the existing private healthcare delivery system. But, the existing private healthcare delivery system has neither reduced healthcare's costs nor provided comprehensive, quality, and easily available healthcare services for those patients unable to pay for them. True! However, by adopting the six changes proposed in this book to REGULATE the existing private delivery system, both can be achieved.

11

Training Future Physicians

The reasons for the impending physician shortage and curtailed healthcare service have been discussed. But, why recovering from a shortage of physicians will take at least twelve years to train additional physicians, and why the ability of those who become physicians may have to be questioned has not been discussed.

Training a physician begins with a four years premed college curriculum followed by four years in medical school. The first two years in medical school are primarily classroom studies learning the basic sciences (anatomy, histology, pathology, biochemistry, pharmacology, physiology, laboratory test results, physical diagnosis, endocrinology, etc.) During the last two years, the student applies those basic sciences to learn their clinical sciences—how to examine, diagnosis, and treat patients. Following medical school's four years most graduating physicians enter a hospital's resident training program to specialize in one area of medicine or surgery. Completing the residency program requires an additional four or five years. Together, all the training requires twelve years to train a physician. Frequently, following college, medical school, and a residency program, physicians spend an additional year or two in a fellowship program learning more about their specialty.

In addition to the twelve years required to train future physicians, there are four reasons why the abilities of those physicians may have to be questioned. First, will the best of our youth be attracted to become those future physicians? Second, will those future physicians be provided adequate training programs? Third, during their training, will physicians continue to request fewer nights and weekends on-call schedules? Four, will the need to supply more physicians to fill a physician shortage result in training programs reducing the time required to become a physician?

First, will the best of our youth be attracted to become our future physicians? The fact that neither government's (Medicare) nor the managed healthcare industry's policies have been physician friendly has been discussed. Furthermore, the probability government and the managed healthcare industry will control the future healthcare delivery system is not a career choice incentive for those thinking about becoming physicians. In addition, the frivolous malpractice lawsuits are not career incentives. Without a friendly physician practice environment and career incentives, the best of our youth will not be attracted to become physicians.

Second, will future physician training programs provide adequate training opportunities? Teaching the basic sciences in classrooms during the student's first two years in medical school will not be a challenge for future physician training programs. However, acquiring enough patients for third and fourth year medical students and for resident physicians to examine and treat has been, and will continue to be, a training problem,

Acquiring patients for training programs became a problem following the closure of the free clinics and inpatient hospital wards in the early 1970s. Prior to their closure, there were many outpatient clinic patients and inpatient hospital ward patients for students and resident physicians to examine and treat. But, after their closure, those patients had to be replaced with private patients. Acquiring an adequate number of private patients willing to be examined and treated by students and resident physicians has been a problem and will continue to be a challenge for training programs.

Third, will physicians during their training continue to request fewer nights and weekend on-call schedules? Acquiring the knowledge to become a physician requires much reading and study, but learning how to apply that knowledge by examining and treating patients is equally, if not more, important. The more patients examined and treated the better is the physician's training and acquired clinical skills.

Prior to the 1970s, most resident physicians worked five and a half days a week, and they were on call in the hospital every other night and every other weekend. During those years, resident physicians learned how to refresh themselves with a few hours sleep. But they had the opportunity to examine and treat many patients. However, since the 1970s, resident physicians have been requesting, and obtaining, fewer nights and weekends on-call. Those fewer on call schedules limit their opportunity to examine and treat more patients and acquire more clinical skills. An eight to five training program will not produce the best physician. Acquiring the knowledge necessary to pass a written examination does not imply a physician possess the clinical skills required to diagnosis and treat patients. The officer, Major Frank, in the MASH television series, epitomizes the physician with poor clinical skills.

Fourth, will the need to supply more physicians to fill a physician shortage result in training programs reducing the time required to become a physician? As I was preparing to retire, there were medical educators discussing how to reduce the time required to become a physician. Hopefully, this will never become policy.

New Jersey's legislature had proposed a medical education and clinical training program in the mid 1970s that could have become the model for future physician training programs. At the time, I was the Professor and Chairman of a Surgical Department in a local Medical School. My challenge was obtaining enough private patients for my students and resident physicians to examine and treat. Our large city hospital and our hospital's free clinics had closed. I had to search for community hospitals with Medical Staffs willing to allow my students and resident physicians examine and participate in the treatment of their private patients. Also, I needed those Medical Staff members to have the desire to share their knowledge and clinical skills with the students and resident physicians. During my search, I learned of the proposed New Jersey program, and it appeared to offer the solution for my patient problem.

The proposed New Jersey program had the student spending their first two years at the medical school in classrooms learning their basic sciences. During their third and fourth years, the student was to be assigned to an affiliated community hospital to learn their clinical sciences. The Medical Staffs in those community hospitals would become their teachers, and the Medical Staff's private patients would become the patient resource for the students and resident physicians to examine and treat. Those Medical Staff members would be given a curriculum to follow, and they would receive a small stipend for their teaching time. A small cadre of fulltime salaried Medical School physicians would be assigned to the community hospitals to supervise the training programs.

Another positive for the New Jersey program was its ability to reduce the cost of medical education. Teaching students and resident physicians how to examine, diagnosis, and treat patients in the free outpatient clinics and inpatient hospital wards required medical schools to employ fulltime physicians. Their salaries and benefits were a significant expense, and those costs had to be acquired from the medical student's tuition. Replacing most of a Medical School's fulltime and salaried physicians with an affiliated community hospital's Medical staff members who were receiving small stipends for their teaching services would have been much less expensive. The cost of medical education could have been reduced significantly.

Unfortunately, the program was never accepted. Instead of community physicians and their private patients becoming the teachers and patient resource for students and resident physicians in those affiliated community hospitals, the medical school placed salaried fulltime physicians in those hospitals.

Those salaried physicians created two problems. First, they had to compete with the community's private practicing physicians for the community's private patients. This made acquiring private patients for the students and resident physicians to examine and treat more difficult. Second, the competition for those patients forced the community's physicians to withdraw their support for a proposed Veteran's hospital. Although the VA hospital would have provided additional patients for the students and resident physicians to examine and treat, those VA patients would have depleted the community's pool of private patients already being depleted by the Medical School's salaried fulltime physicians.

Training additional physicians to recover from a physician shortage will not be without its problems. In addition to the career incentives necessary to attract the best of our youth to become those physicians, there must be a healthcare delivery system available whose private patients have different diseases and disorders and are willing to have students and resident physicians examine and treat them. Will the career incentives and patients be available?

Addendum I
Wage and Price Controls

During the 1990s, Medicare and the managed healthcare industry became major healthcare insurers, and they began to reduce their provider's reimbursements. But, while reducing their provider's reimbursements, the salaries, benefits, and bonuses paid to their administrators and managers and their profits were increasing. If a healthcare insurer's increasing administrative and management costs and their profits were to be paid by reducing their healthcare provider's reimbursements, a standard had to be established to determine the value of, and to calculate the reimbursements for, all healthcare service. The Provider Reimbursement Formula provides that standard (Chapter 5). But the Formula introduces wage and price controls. A problem? No!

Valid arguments have been offered against wage and price controls, but those arguments pertain to the free market economy. In a free market, consumers have the option of deciding whether or not they want to purchase a service, and they have the option of deciding the price they are willing to pay for the service. In addition, in a free market, consumer purchases influence the demand for, the supply of, and the price of, a service or product. An increasing consumer demand reduces supply and increases price while a decreasing consumer demand increases supply and lowers price.

However, the healthcare delivery system is a different economic system. Patients (consumers) do not have the option of deciding whether or not they want to purchase a medically necessary service or of deciding the price they are willing to pay for the service. They must receive the service, and they must pay whatever is necessary to obtain the service. Furthermore, unlike the free market economy, patient purchases of healthcare's services do not influence the demand for, the supply of, or the price of, those services. Instead, healthcare's providers have determined the demand for, the supply of, and the price of, healthcare's services.

One example of how providers created the demand for, and established the price of, healthcare's services was the government's unsuccessful attempt to reduce healthcare's costs by increasing the number of physicians to encourage competition among them. The government subsidized the expansion of medical schools to enable them to graduate more physicians. In addition, foreign trained physicians were encouraged to enter the United States. But, as the numbers of physicians increased, so did healthcare's costs. Why? Those additional physicians were able to offer their patients additional services regardless of their medical necessity (create demand). Also, those physicians were able to establish their charges for those services (establish the price). As long as healthcare's providers have the ability to arbitrarily create the demand for, and establish the price of, healthcare's services, attempts to reduce the cost of those services by increasing the number of providers will not reduce healthcare's costs. Instead, increasing the number of providers will influence only the quality of the services provided patients.

Another example of how healthcare's providers have been able to create the demand for healthcare's services was the unsuccessful attempts to freeze insurance reimbursements. Although the reimbursements for many services were frozen, healthcare's costs continued to increase. Why? Again, providers were able to compensate for their frozen reimbursements by providing their patients additional services regardless of their medical necessity.

These examples illustrate why the only way to stabilize healthcare's costs and to obtain the necessary reductions in those costs is to have both the wage and price controls contained in the Provider Reimbursement Formula (Chapter 5) and medical necessity monitoring (Chapter 4).

The Provider Reimbursement Formula's wage and price controls offer several benefits. First, they remove an insurer's control of healthcare's "purse strings". Second, they reduce and stabilize the cost of healthcare's services. Third, they are both patient and provider friendly. Fourth, they will preserve the patient and physician friendly private healthcare delivery system. Fifth, by preserving the private healthcare delivery system, the career incentives necessary to attract the best of our youth to consider becoming physicians are maintained and the impending physician shortage is avoided. Sixth, by reducing healthcare's costs, those wage and price controls avoid the curtailment of healthcare's services.

The importance of preserving a private healthcare delivery system and it's career incentives requires those incentives be repeated. They are:

1. The opportunity to be independent practitioners in a fee-for-service private healthcare delivery system rather than salaried employees of a National Health Service whose future depends on the whims of another government bureaucracy.

2. The opportunity to receive reimbursements for their services established by the Provider Reimbursement Formula rather than established by an insurer.

3. The opportunity to have 90% of healthcare's dollars spent purchasing healthcare's services for patients (the indemnity insurance industry—Addendum V) rather than 50%, or more, of those dollars spent supporting another government bureaucracy and the infrastructure of the managed healthcare industry.

4. The opportunity to treat patients who have had the opportunity to choose their providers.

5. The opportunity to establish their patient's service needs without a third party's approval prior to the patient receiving the service.

6. The opportunity to have the monitoring of, and the challenges to, the medical necessity of their services made by peers who are qualified to make those challenges.

7. The opportunity to have the cost of their malpractice insurance significantly reduced.

8. The opportunity to offer their patients more comprehensive, quality, and easily available healthcare services at a lower cost than those offered by either a HMO or a National Health Service.

Allowing healthcare's insurers to continue to control healthcare's "purse strings" and determine the value of healthcare's services, and their reimbursements, is no longer acceptable. Instead, a standard is necessary to establish those values and reimbursements. The Provider Reimbursement Formula is the standard, and its wage and price controls offer several benefits. The endorsement of both the Provider Reimbursement Formula and its wage and price controls is recommended.

Addendum II
Healthcare is not a Business

During the 1960s, the unprecedented amount of unregulated health and hospital insurance money flowing into the healthcare delivery system attracted businesspersons and their investors. They saw the opportunity to obtain large profits. However, they were not able to enter healthcare until legislation created the managed healthcare industry in the mid 1970s. Since entering healthcare, they have attempted to manage the delivery of healthcare's services as a business system. But, they have not been successful, and they will continue to be unsuccessful. The healthcare delivery system is a different system, and the following are some of those differences.

A successful business has an operating budget. However, the variable costs associated with evaluating and treating the broad spectrum of healthcare's many different diseases and disorders make adhering to a budget difficult, if not impossible. Also, attempts to maintain a budget by denying patients their services before they received them was not successful. Those denials compromised too many treatment programs.

A business has a management team who designs a business plan and who directs the company's resources to achieve the goals of the business plan. In contrast, healthcare has a variety of "management teams" called physicians and other healthcare providers. They design many different plans to treat healthcare's many different diseases and disorders and direct the use of healthcare's many different resources to achieve the goals of those treatment plans.

There is a difference between a business consumer and a healthcare consumer. The business consumer has three options. First, they have the option of deciding if they want to purchase the business service. Second, they have the option of deciding the price they are willing to pay for the service. Third, they have the option of going to different providers in search of a better price for the same service, and they can be assured the quality of the same service will be the same at all of the different providers. For example, the quality of the same model new automobile is the same at all automobile dealerships.

In contrast, the healthcare consumer has neither the option of deciding if they want to purchase a necessary healthcare service nor the option of deciding the price they are willing to pay for the service. They must receive the service, and they must pay whatever is necessary to acquire the service. In addition, although the healthcare consumer has the option of going to different providers seeking a better price for the same service, they can not be assured the quality of the same service provided by different providers will be the same. There are doctors, and there are doctor's doctors. The doctor's doctor is the doctor other doctors recognized as providing superior services and whose services they seek for themselves and for their families.

A business decision determines how best to make a business service more attractive to consumers. In contrast, there is no need to make a necessary healthcare service more attractive to consumers (patients). The consumers (patients) must have the service.

A business decision determines how best to have a business service generate a profit in order for the business to remain in business. In contrast, healthcare decisions determine how best to have healthcare's services maintain and restore health. Remaining in business is not a problem for the healthcare industry.

Both the quality and the availability of a business service can be modified, but neither the quality nor the availability of a necessary healthcare service can be modified.

Increasing the cost of a business service may discourage its purchase. However, increasing the cost of a healthcare service will not discourage its purchase. Patients must have the service.

Business services can be restricted to only those consumers who can afford to purchase them, and the charges for those services can be adjusted to whatever the consumer is willing to pay. However, necessary healthcare services cannot be restricted to only those consumers (patients) who can afford to purchase them, and the charges for those services cannot be adjusted to whatever the consumer (patient) is willing to pay.

Discussing the differences between business systems and the healthcare delivery system are not intended to be critical of the business community. The discussion amplifies only why the two systems are different and why the attempts to manage healthcare as a business system has not been successful, and will continue to be unsuccessful.

Addendum III
The HMOs, Patients Beware!

HMO is the acronym for Hand the Money Over.

Yes, the managed healthcare industry's HMOs are removing billions of dollars from the healthcare delivery system:
a. To pay investors dividends,
b. To pay its management generous salaries and benefits.
c. To pay expensive marketing and advertising costs, and
d. To pay other administrative and operating expenses.

Those billions of dollars would be better spent purchasing healthcare's services for patients in a regulated private healthcare delivery system whose insurer is the indemnity insurance industry.

What is an HMO? An HMO is neither an insurance company nor a healthcare provider. It is a business! It buys and sells healthcare's services for a profit. It contracts with a variety of healthcare's providers to buy their services at a specified price, and it manages the sale (distribution) of those services by controlling when, where, and from whom their enrollees receive them.

In contrast, a private indemnity insurance company is an insurance company. It neither buys nor sells healthcare's services. Instead, it is a broker. It transfers the money it receives from its policyholder's premiums to the providers who have provided those policyholders services. In addition, it does not control when, where, or from whom its policyholders receive their services.

A frequently asked question is, "Since HMOs offer less expensive premiums, isn't this an example of an HMO's ability to save healthcare's dollars? No! No!! No!!!

HMOs have been able to offer less expensive premiums because:

1. They were able to restrict their enrollments to the 80% of the population with no disabilities or chronic illnesses.

2. They have been able to deny their enrollees services.

3. They have been able to control their reimbursements to the providers of their healthcare services,

4. They have been able to control when, where, and from whom their enrollees receive their services.

In contrast, a private indemnity insurance company has more expensive premiums because:

1. They enroll everyone, including individuals with preexisting disabilities, diseases, and chronic illnesses.

2. They do not deny their policyholders any services.

3. They do not control their provider's reimbursements.

4. They do not control when, where, and from whom their policyholders receive their services.

The HMO industry was able to establish itself by having the ability to offer less expensive premiums. Initially, HMOs did not enroll patients with either disabilities or chronic illnesses. Those patients create 65% to 70% of healthcare's costs, and enrolling only "healthy" individuals offered the HMO industry a significant cost advantage over competing private indemnity insurance companies. Those companies were accepting individuals with disabilities and chronic illnesses. Therefore, an indemnity insurance company's service costs were at least 65% greater than a HMO's service costs. Or, HMOs could anticipate saving 65% of an indemnity insurance company's service costs.

If an indemnity insurance company's service costs required a $6,000 premium, at least 65% of the $6,000 premium was the cost of the company's services to its policyholders with disabilities and chronic illnesses. 65% of $6,000 is $3,900. The remaining $2,100 is the cost of the indemnity insurance company's services to its policyholders with no disabilities or chronic illnesses.

Since the HMO industry avoided enrolling individuals with disabilities and chronic illnesses, the industry could anticipate spending only $2,100 for its "healthy" enrollee's service costs. HMOs would not have to spend the $3,900 the indemnity insurance company had to spend to provide its policyholders with disabilities and chronic illnesses their services.

If the competing HMO industry's premium was only $5,000, after spending the $2,100 for its "healthy" enrollees' services, the HMO had a $2,900 profit remaining from its $5,000 premium. Or, because of its selective enrollment policies, the HMO industry was able to obtain a $2,900 profit from a $5,000 premium while the indemnity insurance company was unable to obtain a profit from its $6,000 premium.

How wrong you were to think the HMO industry was conceived to benefit the public by providing a more efficient delivery system to save healthcare's dollars.

During the 1980s, the HMO industry created both competition and cost problems for the indemnity insurance industry. The need for the indemnity insurance industry to provide services to its policyholders with disabilities and chronic illnesses made its premiums more expensive than the competing HMO's premiums. Also, an increasing number of the "healthy" indemnity insurance industry's policyholders were enrolling in the HMOs and causing additional cost problems for the indemnity insurance industry. A portion of those "healthy" individual's premiums had been used to pay for the more expensive services required by the indemnity insurance industry's policyholders with disabilities and chronic illnesses. The loss of those "healthy" policyholder's premiums and the need to continue to offer the more expensive services to its policyholders with disabilities and chronic illnesses required the cost of the indemnity insurance industry's premiums to increase. Over several decades, those increasing premium costs made them less and less competitive with the HMO industry's premiums. By the 1990s, the indemnity insurance industry was no longer an effective competitor among healthcare's insurers. HMOs had become major healthcare insurers, and with no competition, they began to accept enrollees with disabilities and chronic illnesses. But, as the number of those enrollees increased, the cost of the HMO's premiums increased.

The Future of HMOs.

As discussed in the Preface, those members in Congress seeking a National Health Service created the HMO industry in the mid 1970s to destroy both the private insurance industry and the private healthcare delivery system. In the 1990s, those members in Congress seeking a National Health Service proposed the Patient's Bill of Rights legislation to destroy the HMO industry. Its destruction would have created both a healthcare insurer and a healthcare delivery system problem for those HMO enrollees. Those insurer and delivery system problems could be used to influence those enrollees to offer their support for a National Health Service. In addition, government wanted the HMO industry's infrastructure to become the delivery system for its National Health Service. Fortunately, neither the Patient's Bill of Rights legislation nor the National Health Service legislation was successful.

Presently, the greatest threat to the HMO industry would be the adoption of the proposed six changes to regulate the existing private healthcare delivery system. The HMO industry's expensive infrastructure would have difficulty competing with a regulated private healthcare delivery system whose major insurer was the restored indemnity insurance industry. (Addendum V)

Would the public benefit from a HMO controlled healthcare delivery system? No. Why? In addition to being neither physician nor patient friendly, HMOs have not been able to provide a better delivery system than, nor improve the services offered by, the existing private healthcare delivery system. The industry's interest in healthcare has been, and remains, profits. To obtain those profits, the industry controls the distribution of, and the cost of, the services their enrollees receive. Neither is patient friendly.

Distribution is controlled by telling their enrollees when, where, and from whom they will receive their services. HMO enrollees are required to obtain their services, as well as their referrals to other HMO "approved" consultants, from their HMO's primary care physicians. Costs are controlled by the HMO's ability to establish the value of, and their reimbursements for, healthcare provider's services. Over several decades, those distribution and cost controls have not benefited either their enrollees or the physicians providing their enrollee's services. They have benefited only the industry's management and its investors.

Furthermore, if the HMO industry were to become the delivery system for a National Health Service, neither patients nor healthcare's providers would benefit. Only the HMO industry and the politician would benefit. An HMO controlled delivery system provides the HMO industry profits, and a National Health Service provides politicians both the political power of a large voting block and increased public dependency on government.

Based on my short tenure as the Medical Director of an HMO, the public would be foolish to expect a HMO controlled healthcare delivery system to benefit them. My observation of a HMO is it is a profit driven business. Its managers think of their enrollees as numbers and liabilities; they think of physicians as their service providers; and they believe all physician's services are negotiable—the lowest bid would take preference over quality. Furthermore, the cost of an HMO's management, administration, and other operational and infrastructure expenses would prevent the HMO industry from offering the comprehensive and easily available healthcare services offered by a regulated private healthcare delivery system.

My hope is the managed healthcare industry will never become the primary healthcare delivery system in the United States.

Addendum IV
Physician, cure yourself

The unchallenged ability to misuse health and hospital insurance during the 1960s provided physicians unprecedented incomes, and those incomes were the only reason many individuals became physicians. Unfortunately, after becoming physicians, those physicians abandoned their profession's traditional mores and its previously effective organizational structure, discipline, and leadership. Arrogance, insularity, and avarice characterized many of those physicians. In 2007, those physicians, as well as every other physician, need to acknowledge how they have misused health and hospital insurance and how those misuses have changed themselves, their profession, and the public's image of physicians. Otherwise, both government and the managed healthcare industry will continue to be their masters, and the public will continue to support government's and the managed healthcare industry's control of the healthcare delivery system.

Most physicians practicing medicine in 2007 are not aware of how health and hospital insurance has been misused or of how those misuses have changed both themselves and their profession. They entered medicine after the 1970s, and they never knew the practice of medicine prior to health and hospital insurance.

Those physicians are not aware that prior to those insurance programs physicians had to ask their patients to pay for their services from their pocketbooks; or aware physicians required several years to establish a private practice with enough private patients capable of paying their fees; or aware physicians never expected to make the incomes insurance has been providing physicians since the 1960s; or aware physicians were expected to provide free medical and surgical services to patients unable to pay for them; or aware physicians were expected to become members of their local and national Medical or Osteopathic Societies; or aware membership in those Societies was necessary to obtain malpractice insurance and hospital appointments; or aware physicians expected their professional and ethical behavior to be monitored by those Societies; or aware those Societies could discipline and censor physicians. There is much they do not know about their profession's traditions.

Medicine's organizational problems began to surface during the 1960s. The practice of medicine was becoming more specialized, and membership in the many different specialty organizations became more important than membership in local and national Medical and Osteopathic Societies. Professional insularity prevailed, and the organizational maze created by the agendas of the many different specialty organizations made obtaining consensus among physicians impossible. "Organized medicine" became a misnomer, and a leadership vacuum, as well as discipline issues, quickly followed the absence of organization.

In 2005, all practicing physicians are members of one or more specialty organizations, but less than 35% are members of their profession's local and national Societies. With less than a 35% membership, those local and national Societies offer no effective leadership. Those leadership issues and problems will continue until D.O. (Osteopathic) and M.D. physicians recognize their need to become one professional organization. In 2007, there is no reason for their continued professional separation. Also, the need for all physicians to achieve effective organizational consensus is a compelling reasons for D.O. and M.D. physicians to become one professional organization.

A historical perspective will assist both D.O. and M.D. physicians, as well as the public, to understand the reasons for the professional separation of M.D. and D.O. physicians and why the continued separation is absurd.

During World War II, the military did not recognize Osteopathy, and D.O. physicians were not drafted. As the draft removed more and more M.D. physicians form each community, the D.O. physicians became the country's family physicians. After World War II, D.O. physicians wanted professional recognition. They obtained it, and their students were required to pass the same State Board Medical Examinations the M.D. physicians were required to pass.

During the 1950s and 1960s, many M.D. physicians were becoming specialists, but D.O. physicians had no specialty training programs to attend. In addition, they were not accepted into M.D. specialty training programs. But, in the late 1960s, M.D. specialty training programs began to accept D.O. physicians, and those D.O. physicians became specialists with the same training as their M. D.

colleagues. In time, D.O. specialists initiated training programs in their Osteo-pathic hospitals. Since the 1980s, there is no longer any training differences between D.O. and a M.D. physicians. However, among both D.O. and the M.D. physicians, there remains the doctor and the doctor's doctor. My internist had been a D.O. physician.

In addition to organizational problems, physicians acquired leadership problems during the 1970s. One was their failure to sponsor HMOs. Osteopathic and Medical Society sponsorship would have been appropriate to insure patients enrolling in HMOs received the correct medical and surgical services. If busi-nesspersons were to control HMOs, they would be unable to make the appropri-ate decisions about either the quality, the comprehensiveness, or the necessity of their enrollee's services. Unfortunately, at the time, there was no physician sup-port for HMOs. Why? Too many physicians were profiting from their misuse of unregulated health and hospital insurance programs, and they were opposed to any delivery system (HMO) that would threaten their continued and unchal-lenged misuse of those insurances.

Other examples of leadership issues among both M.D. and D.O. physicians in the 1970s were their failures to sponsor hospice programs, outpatient surgical centers, multidisciplinary cancer treatment centers, and to maintain control of hospitals. I recall the failed attempts to initiate a hospice in the early 1970s. Medicare was identifying and eliminating unnecessary Medicare hospital admis-sions and the days following those admissions. Those denials were creating many unoccupied hospital beds. Hospitals did not support the Hospice program because they wanted their unoccupied beds to be occupied with those patients with terminal illness. Unfortunately, at the same time, physicians were slowly abandoning their hospital management responsibilities, and they offered no chal-lenges to their hospital's failure to support the hospice concept of treating patients with terminal illnesses.

In the 1970s, another leadership issue was the failure of physicians to support out patient surgical centers. A colleague had participated in starting one of the first surgical outpatient facility in Phoenix, Arizona. My attempts to have our hospital start an outpatient surgical center failed. The hospital wanted those surgical patients to use the hospital's operating rooms. Again, there was no physician sup-port for outpatient surgical centers until they learned they could profit from their ownership of those centers.

Another leadership issue in the 1970s was the failure of physicians to support community and regional multidisciplinary cancer treatment centers. During the 1960s, many new drugs were being developed to treat cancer patients, and new Xray machines were developed capable of penetrating radiation deeply into the body's tissues to more effectively treat cancer patients. In addition, new surgical procedures and anesthesia advances were making more effective surgical procedures possible. To learn how to obtain the maximum benefit from those new treatments, patients needed to be entered into treatment protocols. Protocols outlined specific treatment programs, and the best way to enter patients into, and to evaluate the results of, those protocols was to have multidisciplinary cancer treatment centers. Otherwise, cancer patients were being sent from one physician's office to another without any coordination of, or effective evaluation of, the treatment's results. All community physicians and their patients would have been able to participate in those centers. However, neither hospitals nor physicians supported the adoption of community multidisciplinary cancer treatment centers prior to the 1980s.

Another leadership issue was the failure of physicians to maintain control of the charitable community hospital systems. In the late 1960s and into the 1970s, the increasing number of patients with health insurance was offering physicians the opportunity to spend more time treating private patients in their offices. As their office practices increased, physicians began to withdraw from their previous hospital administration responsibilities. Unfortunately, while physicians were withdrawing, legislation was creating the managed healthcare industry in the mid 1970s. Those businesspersons quickly assumed those hospital administration responsibilities, and over a decade, those businesspersons changed our country's charitable community hospital systems into investor owned and profit driven multi-hospital systems.

Concerns about the loss of physician leadership within hospitals gave rise to the American Academy of Medical Directors in the 1970s. The Academy offered training programs for physicians to learn hospital management, and the Academy encouraged physicians to accept hospital administration responsibilities.

In addition to their organizational and leadership issues, physicians began to acquire discipline issues during the 1970s. Two examples are physician advertising and selling products from their offices. Neither was allowed prior to the

1970s. To do so would have resulted in the physician being censored by their local Society. If censored, the physician would have a problem obtaining malpractice insurance, hospital privileges, and membership in many Societies and specialty organizations.

The problem with advertising is it does not offer patients the opportunity to obtain the best services. A patient's physician knows the needs of their patients and the abilities of other healthcare providers to whom the physician would refer their patients. Therefore, a patient's physician should be making their patient's service referrals, and not advertising attracting patients. Also, selling products from physician's offices encourages the sale of those items regardless of their need or medical necessity.

As medicine's mores began to break down during the 1960s and into the 1970s, the number of physicians advertising and selling appliances increased rapidly. Otolaryngologists (ENT) began to sell hearing aids; Orthopedists began to sell rehabilitation services and appliances; Ophthalmologists (Eye) began to sell eyeglasses; and other specialties began to sell other items. Physician advertising was rampant.

A fact! Physician advertising and selling products from their offices is not defensible by suggesting they benefit patients. They are profit driven, and neither is professional nor serves our profession honorably.

Is it possible for physicians to cure themselves? Repeating what has been discussed, there will always be a payment system to pay for healthcare's services, and there will always be a delivery system to offer patients their healthcare services. But, in the next decade, will the provider system have physicians, and other healthcare professional, who have come from the best of our youth and who have the ability to provide the public quality, comprehensive, and easily available healthcare services?

The provider system's future depends on the action, if any, physicians take in 2007. Can physicians restructure their profession? Can they provide the leadership necessary to recruit their colleague's participation in eliminating insurance misusages, reducing healthcare's cost to 8% to 9% of the GNP, and providing services to those patients unable to pay for them? Will physicians adopt the six changes as their agenda to restructure the practice of medicine? Those six changes provide the agenda physicians need to proactively challenge their adversaries. In addition, adopting the six changes would recruit the public's and the business community's support for physicians controlling and managing our country's future healthcare delivery system.

Eliminating insurance misusages, providing the necessary reductions in healthcare's costs, and providing services to those unable to pay for them will attract public support for the six changes. Providing an alternative healthcare delivery system capable of reducing the cost of every employer's healthcare benefits will attract the business community's support for the six changes.

Hopefully, the six changes will become the agenda to restructure the practice of medicine. Although the six changes will attract public and business community support for physicians, physicians can anticipate several challenges as they advance their agenda. One challenge will be overcoming the public's impression that physicians have become avarice, insular, and arrogant.

Another challenge will be those individuals who are indifferent to healthcare's increasing costs. They are indifferent because they do not pay those costs. Their insurance pays those costs. Also, someone else pays for, and provides them, their insurance. As long as the public does not have to contribute towards the cost of their healthcare services, they will remain indifferent to those costs and resist any changes in the healthcare delivery system that might deny them the unnecessary services they may be receiving.

Another challenge for physicians will be the 80% of the public who are healthy. Since they rarely have the need for healthcare's services, they rarely, if ever, think about the future healthcare delivery system or the probability their healthcare services will become increasingly difficult to obtain. Those healthy individuals will have to be reminded SOME TYPE OF DISORDER, DISEASE, OR CHRONIC ILLNESS IS IN EVERYONE'S FUTURE. At that time, both their healthcare delivery system and the physicians providing their delivery system's services will be extremely important to them and to their families.

Another challenge will be having the public become aware of the probability the abilities and numbers of their future physician may have to be questioned. Their physicians may not have come from the best of our youth, and they may not have received the best training. The public will have to be reminded of the different clinical and surgical abilities of "Hawkeye" and Major Frank in the TV series MASH. "Hawkeye" was the doctor's doctor while Major Frank had limited clinical and surgical abilities.

If more "Hawkeyes" than Major Franks are to be available to provide the public's future healthcare services, the public will have to be reminded that their future healthcare delivery system must offer the career incentives necessary to attract the best of our youth to become those "Hawkeyes". Also, they will need to be reminded that the delivery system offering the best opportunity to have those career incentives is a regulated private healthcare delivery system.

Anther challenge for physicians will be those patients with existing diseases, disorders, and chronic illnesses. They generate most of healthcare's costs, and they have two characteristics. One is many of them have an existing dependency on government. The other characteristic is most of them are elderly.

Existing government programs provide health and hospital services to many patients with chronic illnesses. Those individuals may be difficult to convince a regulated private healthcare delivery system would be best for our country. Also, elderly patients are facing two problems. One is an increasing number of them are living longer than the funds available to support them. After twenty years in retirement, many fixed incomes become inadequate. The other elderly problem is many have to enter expensive nursing homes and other assisted living facilities. In the next decade, an increasing number of elderly patients will find themselves increasingly dependent on others. They can be expected to lobby Congress for government assistance. Although their government assistance will continue, physicians will need to explain to those elderly, and to those patients with existing illnesses, how a regulated private healthcare delivery will reduce healthcare's costs and how those reductions will benefit them.

Another challenge for physicians will be instructing the business community about the benefits of a regulated private healthcare delivery system. The business community's employee healthcare benefits have become an enormous cost burden, and no alternative healthcare plan has been proposed to reduce those costs. The business community would be foolish not to attempt to pass those expensive employee healthcare benefits on to a National Health Service.

Businesses need to understand that the six changes to regulate the existing private healthcare delivery system can provide the alternative healthcare delivery system they have been seeking. It will provide the necessary reductions in their employee's healthcare benefits costs. For example, within three years, the six changes could reduce healthcare's costs by at least 30%, and within five years, up to 40%. A business with 3,000 employees could anticipate having their employee health benefit costs reduced by at least $3,000 to $4,000 for each employee within three years. Their savings would be nine to twelve million dollars. Support for the regulated private healthcare delivery system proposed in this book will benefit the business community.

Physician: Your Future?

Are practicing D.O. and M.D. physicians aware of their profession's, dilemma? Have they given any thought to, or share any concern for, what may be ahead for both themselves and their colleagues in the next decade? Are they aware of their immediate need for proactive policies to restore public confidence in the ability of physicians to effectively manage healthcare's cost and service availability problems?

The paraphrased comment of a golfing friend, for whom I have great respect, moved me to finish writing this book. He started and owned a large business that employs several hundred people, and his wife was recently hospitalized. "Lindsay, what the hell has happened to your profession? I use to have great respect for physicians. They were dedicated to, and seemed interested in, their patients. If I had managed my business the arrogant way my wife's physicians managed her, I would have been out of business."

Physicians must acknowledge the behavior of too many physicians have lost both the public's and the business community's support for physicians controlling and managing the healthcare delivery system. The best way to restore that confidence is to restructure their profession. Otherwise, the public and the business community will, within this decade, seek relief for their healthcare problems from government and the managed healthcare industry. Neither will be patient nor physician friendly.

    a.   My suggestion for professional restructuring is:

        1.   Both the D.O. and M.D. physician become one professional organization. In 2007, both D.O. and M.D. physicians practice medi-

cine. The word Osteopathy should be eliminated slowly. There is a precedent for eliminating the word Osteopathy. In the early 1900s, Homeopathy was eliminated. Those physicians who had practiced Homeopathy (my grandfather) became medical practitioners.

2. The existing National, State, and local Osteopathic and Medical Societies become one Medical Society. The need for leadership is a compelling reason for both Societies to become one professional Society.

3. To restore consensus among all physicians, the many agendas of the different specialty organizations need to be included in the agendas of the reorganized national, state, and local Medical Societies. To accomplish this, those Medical Societies will function as holding companies like those in business. Each of the specialty organizations will continue to function independently and represent their specialty's interests; however, each of those specialties will have a representative on the Executive Committees of the reorganized National, State, and local Medical Societies. This will provide each specialty representation in those Medical Societies and the opportunity to have those Medical Societies provide additional support for their agendas when necessary.

Existing National, State, and local Medical and Osteopathic Societies have lost membership over recent decades because those Societies have not been able to represent the agendas of the different specialty organizations. Too many physicians have said. "Neither the AMA nor my local Medical Society have done anything for my specialty. Why should I join them?"

Following their professional restructuring, my suggestion is those Medical Societies adopt the six changes as their agenda to eliminate health and hospital insurance misusages, provide the necessary reductions in healthcare's costs, and provide facilities to offer patients, unable to purchase their services, the opportunity to receive them.

Physician, cure yourself!

The comprehensiveness, the quality, and the availability of our country's future healthcare services as well as the number, and the abilities, of our future physicians will depend on the action physicians take now.

Addendum V
Healthcare's Insurers

The many benefits offered by adopting the six changes to regulate the existing private healthcare delivery system have been discussed. However, the importance of the type of insurance program paying for the private healthcare delivery system's services has not been discussed.

At this time, government (Medicare) and the managed healthcare industry are major healthcare insurers. But, as discussed previously, both want to control healthcare in addition to being its insurers. An alternative to both of those healthcare insurers is a restored private indemnity insurance industry. The industry's ability to save healthcare dollars would benefit patients, healthcare's providers, and the business community.

An indemnity insurance company neither establishes the value of, nor the reimbursements for, healthcare's services. Also, it does not attempt to control the healthcare delivery system, or establish when, where, or from whom its policyholders receive their services. Instead, an indemnity insurance company functions as a healthcare broker. The money it receives from its policyholders is used to pay the healthcare providers who have provided those policyholders services.

The administrative, management, and other operating costs of the indemnity insurance industry would be much less than the same costs of a National Health service and the managed healthcare industry. Using the existing National, State, and local Depts. of Education as our example, the cost of their administrative bureaucracies is reported to consume about 50% of education's dollars. Only 50%, of education's dollars are available for the classroom and its teachers. The National, State, and local bureaucracies required to administer a National Health Service and the managed healthcare industry would consume an equal amount of healthcare's dollars. The loss of 50% of healthcare's dollars to support those bureaucracies leaves only 50% of those dollars available to purchase services for patients. With only 50% of healthcare dollars available to purchase services, those services would have to be curtailed.

In contrast, the indemnity insurance industry's administrative, management, and operating expenses consume only about 15% of the healthcare dollars their policyholders pay in premiums. 85% of those dollars would be available to purchase healthcare's services for those policyholders. In addition, after the Provider Reimbursement Formula has established the amount of the reimbursements for all of healthcare services, indemnity insurance companies would be competing among themselves the opportunity to attract policyholders. The competition would keep the many indemnity insurance company's administrative costs as low as possible in order for them to remain competitive.

Hopefully, the six changes to regulate a private healthcare delivery system will become the delivery system in the United States, and the indemnity insurance industry will become healthcare's insurer again..

Epilogue

Maintaining a physician and patient friendly healthcare delivery system requires the system to offer the career incentives necessary to attract an adequate number of the best of our youth to become its providers and to have those providers provide quality, comprehensive, and easily available healthcare services.

Hopefully, after reading this book, there are enough independent thinkers among the public and within the business community who understand why neither a National Health Service nor the managed healthcare industry can provide a physician and patient friendly healthcare delivery system, and why a regulated private healthcare delivery system, such as the one proposed in this book, can provide a physician and patient friendly delivery system.

As the public and business community ponder their support for a regulated private healthcare delivery system, they will have to be convinced the practice of medicine will remain an honorable profession and its physicians will continue to believe in the meaning of the serpents on a pole that has been the insignia representing their profession.

When Moses took the Israelites out of Egypt, many became impatient and spoke against God and Moses. In response, God sent poisonous serpents among those people. The serpents bit many of them, and they died. In response to Moses' plea for help, God told Moses to make a serpent, which he did of bronze, and to place the serpent on a pole. When a person is bitten by a poisonous serpent, they are to look at the serpent on the pole, and they will recover.

In the next decade, will patients and the business community be able to look to the medical profession and to its physicians and have the same expectations as the Israelites had from the bronze serpent on the pole? I hope so.

978-0-595-43303-2
0-595-43303-0